T0194886

Cancer
The Unexpected Gift

Inspirational Stories of Hope and Significance

Dr. J. Patrick Daugherty

AND

Edie Hand

iUniverse, Inc.
New York   Bloomington

iUniverse books may be ordered through booksellers or by contacting:

iUniverse
1663 Liberty Drive
Bloomington, IN 47403
www.iuniverse.com
1-800-Authors (1-800-288-4677)

Because of the dynamic nature of the Internet, any Web addresses or links contained in this book may have changed since publication and may no longer be valid. The views expressed in this work are solely those of the author and do not necessarily reflect the views of the publisher, and the publisher hereby disclaims any responsibility for them.

The Scripture quotations are taken from the Holy Bible: New International Version, 1984, unless stated otherwise. Other versions used include: King James Version (KJV), New American Standard Version (NASV), Amplified (AMP), American Standard Version (ASV), and New King James Version (NKJV).

ISBN: 978-1-4401-8767-4 (sc)
ISBN: 978-1-4401-8768-1 (ebook)
ISBN: 978-1-4401-8769-8 (hc)

Library of Congress Control Number: 2009911279

Printed in the United States of America

iUniverse rev. date: 01/22/2010

Keynote: Dr. J. Patrick Daugherty, medical oncologist, joins with Edie Hand, three-time cancer survivor, to provide inspiriting stories of faith, hope, and significance.

Endorsements of *Cancer: The Unexpected Gift*

"An exceptional collection of inspired stories that illustrate important ways to turn a potential trauma into life-reinforcing hope."
 —Dr. Judy Kuriansky, world-renowned clinical psychologist, TV and radio commentator, and author of *The Complete Idiot's Guide to a Healthy Relationship*

"Oncologists are trained to know the physical and emotional effects of cancer for their patients. We hear firsthand the patient stories and the stories of their families. Dr. Patrick Daugherty and Edie Hand together as physician and patient have portrayed the perfect blend of encompassing both sides of the mirror, personally and scientifically."
 —Luis F. Pineada, MD, MSHA, PC, founder of Cooking with Cancer, Inc.

"The book offers the reader a new perspective on cancer patient survivorship. Cancer patients, their families, caregivers, and physicians will be uplifted by the personal accounts of faith, hope, and service discussed in this very readable book. Each personal vignette is prefaced by a short medical description of the illness and is followed by an inspirational message plus an appropriate poem, literary quote, or scriptural passage—this is a very effective way to provide the reader with a stand-alone educational and spiritual lesson."
 —Paul Engstrom, MD, senior member and senior vice president, Population Science Division, and medical director, Fox Chase Network, Fox Chase Cancer Center, Philadelphia, PA

"The authors present encouraging stories of men, women, and children that have traveled a journey with cancer. It is worthwhile reading for patients diagnosed with cancer and for families of patients. These are powerful, moving stories from a clinician with a real heart."
 —Harold G. Koenig, MD, codirector of the Center for Spirituality, Theology, and Health at Duke University Medical Center, and professor of psychiatry and behavioral sciences, and associate professor of medicine, Duke University, Durham, NC

"Platitudes are statements packed with unlived triteness. Testimonies are realities spoken by men and women who have 'been there, done that, and have the scars to prove it.' *The Unexpected Gift* is itself an unexpected gift to those who have heard the diagnosis of cancer and to caregivers who want desperately to help them cope."

—Haddon Robinson, PhD, the Harold John Ockenga Distinguished Professor of Preaching, Gordon-Conwell Theological Seminary, South Hamilton, MA

"These are powerful individual stories."

—John R. Durant, MD, former director, Comprehensive Cancer Center, University of Alabama in Birmingham, and Fox Chase Cancer Center, Philadelphia, PA, and former president, American Society of Clinical Oncology

"The most dreaded word in the English language is the word 'cancer.' The three greatest helps that its victims can experience when it strikes are faith in God, a caring, compassionate, skilled oncologist, and the comfort and testimony of one who has already experienced it. These three are merged so beautifully and empathetically in *The Unexpected Gift*. Having known and observed his life and service for nearly forty years, I know Dr. Patrick Daugherty's contribution to his inspiration 'gift' springs from unselfish devotion, a generous spirit, and a sincere desire to help as many people as possible."

—Dr. David L. Eubanks, president emeritus, Johnson Bible College, Knoxville, TN

"In the often heartbreaking world of oncology Dr. Patrick Daugherty shows that suffering can lead to the most surprising insights. The question of human misery has always been one of the most troubling in Christendom. Where is God when people are suffering? Dr. Daugherty takes us inside the dark hours of a cancer diagnosis to reveal some of the most beautiful and startling lessons in the human experience. I recommend this book to anyone who thinks that suffering has no meaning."

—Dr. Paul Conn, president, Lee University, Cleveland, TN

"It has been such an uplifting experience that you have shared these patients' stories. I am continually reminded that the patients so often thought of as 'dying' are really the most alive of us all. These stories make this so clear."

—Dr. K. Lemone Yielding, dean emeritus, Graduate School of Biomedical Sciences, University Texas, Galveston, TX; physician, Northwest Alabama Cancer Center

Dedication

This book is dedicated to our family members who have been diagnosed with cancer.

****

Dorothy Mae Jack Daugherty: metastatic breast cancer
William Benjamin Daugherty: metastatic head and neck cancer
Ora Lee Daugherty: lung cancer
Ellen Jack Hunt: ovarian cancer
Curtis Jack: prostate cancer

and

Special friend: Debbie Maupin Byous: lung cancer and lymphoma
She was diagnosed and lost her courageous battle with cancer during the writing of this book.

****

and

Terry Blackburn: brain cancer
Guy Blackburn: prostate cancer

****

and

To those still suffering, and those overcoming suffering.

Contents

The Whole World Came to a Complete Stop. Austin's mother tells his story. At age two he was diagnosed with acute lymphoblastic leukemia. After more than three years of chemotherapy, he remains in remission. She received the gift of living one day at a time.

My Life Was Surreal; I Could Not Believe I Had Cancer. Annette had two teenage children and worked at a cancer clinic as a laboratory technician when she discovered she had breast cancer. She now ministers to individuals that share her disease. She received the gift of a new perspective.

Searching for Answers. Employed in the metal recycling industry, Ken survived metastatic colon cancer before he developed prostate cancer, which later spread to his bones. He searched for answers and found significance in his life. He received the gift of service to others.

I Turned It Over to God. Maudie was a grandmother when she was found to have lung cancer, which had spread to her brain. Despite all odds, she continues to enjoy life after nine years and inspires others in the community. She received the gift of surrender to God.

Worry About Nothing; Pray About Everything. As a young mother, Head Start teacher, and children's ministry director, Pam's life changed with the diagnosis of squamous cell cancer of the head and neck. Seventeen years after her initial treatment, she continues her battle against many of the side effects which occurred a decade or more after treatment. She received the gift of no worry.

Using the Most Powerful Medicine. Charles, a hospital administrator familiar with prostate cancer, knew his prognosis was not good. He continues to fight metastatic prostate cancer after ten years and looks forward to his future home. He received the gift of spiritual transformation.

A Feeling of Peace Took Over. Teena was twenty-one when she was diagnosed with Hodgkin's lymphoma. Because of the chemotherapy, there was a possibility she could not have children. Today, she has three precious daughters and works in her physicians' office. She received the gift of inspiring others.

Facing the Valley. Colon cancer did not stop Lynda, a musician and director of a children's choir. She continues her treatments and church activities as she inspires her family and friends. She received the gift of acceptance.

Feeling Lucky. Recently unemployed by the outsourcing of jobs, Mary, a young single mom, faced a lung cancer diagnosis. After the initial treatment, the cancer metastasized to her brain. Three years into treatment, she recently celebrated her son's graduation from high school. She received the gift of beneficial attitude.

This Is the End of My Life. Diagnosed with advanced breast cancer, Willie felt hopeless. But she underwent treatment, her hope renewed, and she continues to share hope about her fifteen-year journey of survival. She received the gift of hope.

We Are in This Together. Retirees Virginia and Wayne enjoy just being together. Virginia's diagnosis of lymphoma and its recurrence have taught the husband and wife team to share more deeply, and they continue to experience a greater love for each other. She received the gift of weness.

Just Another Hill to Climb. As a nurse, Phyllis knows the health-care system. Even with numerous complications from breast cancer treatment, she remains upbeat and spreads her positive attitude to those around her. She received the gift of perseverance.

Foreword

Dr. J. Patrick Daugherty

I love receiving gifts, don't you? But we all know that not all gifts are desired, wanted, or needed. Think of your last Christmas or birthday. There it was—a gift for which you had absolutely no use. As you opened the gift, you probably exhibited emotions you did not feel, simply for the benefit of the gift giver. Over the years, we have learned how to handle this situation: show appreciation for a gift destined to the Salvation Army gift box. Get the idea?

Internet and magazine articles detail how to deal with these problems, telling you what to say to the giver of an unwanted gift and how to dump it or donate it to charity. (If you are lucky to have the sales receipt, you can exchange it for one you like.) According to etiquette expert Leah Ingram, passing the gift to another is viewed as ethical and downright smart, as long as you don't return the gift to the original giver.[1] The activity, termed "regifting" in a 1995 *Seinfeld* episode,[2] can also be called "gifting it forward."

Three-time cancer survivor Edie Hand knows she has received gifts camouflaged as cancer. Together, we tell the stories of twelve ordinary people in northwest Alabama.

The stories describe gifts received by each patient as a result of their cancer diagnosis and treatment.

> Gifts can be camouflaged
> as cancer.

If you are a cancer patient or a family member of a cancer patient, this is about you. The stories are about average people battling a horrible disease. Through their spiritual journeys, we learn about connecting with others and we all benefit from it.

There is power in storytelling. The described journeys, detailing adversities and successes, often mimic a redirection of our own lives. Many of us have experienced such a redirection with a word or a few words rather than a long discourse. In a few pages, patients told these stories to offer hope and redirect lives toward meaning and purpose.

These stories represent spiritual journeys, not doctrines and denominations. Spirituality is belief in a power greater than ourselves, which most people in the United States refer to as God,[3] which gives direction, meaning, and purpose to life. The individuals sharing their stories, individually and collectively, demonstrate that belief. Even if you do not believe in God, you can benefit from these stories from the standpoint of renewed hope and awareness of the need for significance.

> Each individual story is a
> spiritual journey.

Preface

My patients have taught me medicine. More importantly, they have taught me about living. Initially, when patients would tell me about the difficulties and struggles they were undergoing, I would say, "I know" or "I know how you feel." Often patients told me, with all due respect, that I really did not know what they were feeling. Other patients informed me about what helped them in their struggles. Over the years of treating over fifteen thousand cancer patients, many stories are available for almost all medical situations that arise in a medical oncology practice. These narratives are used to demonstrate to newly diagnosed patients how another in a similar situation coped and did well.

The criteria of "doing well" were defined by me: patients who were able to cope with their diagnosis of cancer so their lives took on a newer and somewhat deeper meaning. These patients may not have lived longer, but they lived better. Their lives could provide hope for others who were newly diagnosed. Before I had access to patient stories, I had statistics of groups of patients. The cancer textbooks thrive on them. Although we do live in an information-oriented society, most people are more interested in a hope-oriented world. These twelve stories are not all inclusive. The peer-patient narratives represent only a few ways of effective coping.

> Live better while living
> longer.

> Seek to live in a hope-
> oriented world.

While physicians have a responsibility to inform patients of treatment options, potential risks, and benefits, they also have a responsibility to maintain hope. From a physician's point of view, if I lacked such hopeful stories, I could not enter into a treatment program with some patients. The outlook would be too grim. However, knowing that the possibility of survival and improved quality of life exists, even if transient, hope can be offered to another patient.

Years ago, a patient sought from me a second opinion. I recommended the same treatment program as the other physician, but I emphasized the survival rather than the lack of it. As I was leaving the exam room, she said, "Doctor, at least you didn't take my hope away." I gave her hope that had been removed. In this book, you will read her story.

If you have been diagnosed with cancer, this book is about you. If you are a caregiver, you will learn from these pages. If you are a physician or healthcare professional, you will benefit from the patient narratives. If you are one who is living and often faces difficult times, you will find examples of what has worked for others facing similar situations.

> This book is for you if you are a
> 1. Patient,
> 2. Caregiver,
> 3. Healthcare professional.

This book describes a different approach to the patient-physician relationship. Patients shared their stories. I reviewed them and found within each a gift. These gifts were not new. On the contrary, reading the words written by the patient simply made the gifts more tangible, more real. Having received a gift does not alleviate suffering, but it may facilitate a more favorable response. When tragedy or bad news is part of our lives, we will almost certainly suffer. It is necessary. However, we can often focus on such stories and reach out for the benefit (gift) knowing it is available. It works.

Historically, the physician-patient relationship has implied patient dependence on the professional authority of the physician. Recently, however, the relationship has moved toward shared decision making.

Since the patient initiates the relationship, the authors prefer to term the relationship patient-physician. The novel approach this book takes demonstrates a mutually beneficial relationship. The patient is the recipient of the physician's knowledge and expertise, and the physician benefits from the narrative of the patient. Both the patient and the physician choose what aspects of the relationship to apply to their own lives. The repeated stories of patients, all with a little variation even on the same illness, enhance the physician's ability to practice the art of medicine without sacrificing the application of technology.

In addition to the intention to help, the physician has an intentional willingness to learn, though the patient may have no intentional desire to teach. The patient-physician relationship begins with the physician listening to the patient. With the increase in technology, demands on time, increased numbers of patients, and governmental restraints, the inability or unwillingness of physicians to listen has increased.

As an example, a patient instilled this simple pearl of practice wisdom in my mind when I was an intern. She had been admitted to the hospital dozens of times for repeated urinary tract infections. Usually, since she presented the same way, she had a culture and was admitted or treated with antibiotics. During my first encounter with her, she described her symptoms. She detailed how she felt she needed to urinate, and if she could not, she experienced the sensation of "urinating within herself." Such a statement might have landed her an interview with a psychiatrist, but the appropriate X-ray demonstrated an incompetent valve, which, when corrected, cured her problem of repeated urinary tract infections. That woman, an unintentional teacher, has helped me diagnose the same condition in many other patients.

Acknowledgments

We appreciate the patients who provided their stories. We thank them for their willingness to open their lives and hearts to us and to the readers.

We are grateful to those who reviewed the manuscript, especially Mrs. Carol Rea, Dr. Jean Johnson, Dr. Janet McMullen, and Mrs. Cheryl Milligan. Each provided many helpful comments. We appreciate Mary Ann Gean for transcribing the stories.

And thanks to our spouses, Rebecca Daugherty and Mark Aldridge, for their patience and encouragement. We are grateful for our children who always support our endeavors.

Thanks to Drs. Haddon Robinson and William Messenger of Gordon-Conwell Theological Seminary for their encouragement and assistance during the initial experimental work that demonstrated the power of patients' stories.

We thank Amy Daugherty for the initial design of the cover, and Angela Henderson, Signature Studios, Florence, Alabama, for the final copy. We thank Kristi Poss for her assistance in final edit and marketing plans.

The interviews were conducted and stories generated in 2008.

Introduction

"Cancer is the best thing that ever happened to me," remarked a friend and cancer patient. I asked, somewhat in amazement, "How could that be?" He went on to explain the benefits of his having cancer. His life had taken on a new meaning and purpose. With this direct and powerful statement, from someone with a changed life, I wondered how such a dramatic statement could be made about such a horrible disease. My journey to learn more about spiritual transformation began over twenty years ago, and it has led to this book.

> Cancer is the best thing that ever happened to me.

Actually it may have begun many years prior when I was nine years old. My grandfather, dying of metastatic head and neck cancer, spent time talking to me and other people in his life on the evening he died. I have recalled that conversation many times. Later that evening, he passed away as he sang "Amazing Grace." It is somewhat ironic that the song that brought my grandfather some relief from his suffering was written as a result of heartfelt suffering of a former slave ship captain who became fully aware of his condition before God.

"Cancer is the best thing that ever happened to me," was a statement made not by a delusional individual, but by one who has reaped benefit from a traumatic, life-threatening event. I can easily label such changes as "transformations" because I have known many of the patients prior to their diagnosis of cancer and the patients often described the events in terms of spiritual transformation. Spiritual transformation is counterintuitive to suffering from a secular point of view, but happens from a spiritual point of view as we live out Romans 8:28: "And we know that in all things God works for the good of those who love him, who have been called according to his purpose." It has been the subject of academic inquiry for years, especially since the publication of William James's book (see endnote 8).

"Cancer!" The word is spoken sympathetically and is often whispered. Cancer is one of the most dreaded of diseases. When a person faces a life-threatening diagnosis of cancer, it produces an intense crisis. The news of having cancer often results in strong emotions such as fear, hopelessness, helplessness, and anxiety. The patient experiences extreme vulnerability to the disease, to unfamiliar technology, and to the healthcare delivery system. Lifelong plans change overnight. The diagnosis of cancer confronts the very dimension of living. The life-threatening nature of cancer predisposes one to an increased awareness of one's meaning and purpose of life and often brings spiritual matters to the forefront. Can such a crisis serve as a catalyst for spiritual growth?

> Your plans change
> overnight.

The natural response to suffering is anger, denial, resentment, and blame. Job's wife exhibited a natural response when she told her husband: "Are you still holding on to your integrity? Curse God and die!" (Job 2:9). From Job, we learn that God does not cause suffering, but he does allow it. We also learn that God's children are not immune to suffering, but they are expected to respond to suffering differently. God can use suffering as a tool to bring about Christlikeness in Christians, and in so doing, fulfill Romans 8:28.

Suffering occurs because of natural laws or poor decisions or a combination of both. God set in motion the universe and all the physical laws. God also set in motion laws of relationship and behavior. For example, we know that cigarette smoking causes cancer, yet people still make the decision to smoke. God

> Spirituality often takes on a new meaning after the diagnosis of cancer. God's children are not immune to suffering, but we are expected to respond to it differently.

does not cause a specific patient to get lung cancer. A person develops cancer or other illness in response to the laws governing health. The spiritual law says an event such as cancer may be used by God to bring about the state he desires in us. Is suffering part of a natural law that God uses to get our attention? C. S. Lewis remarked that "pain insists on being attended to. God whispers to us in our pleasures, speaks to us in our conscience, but shouts in our pains: it is His megaphone to rouse a deaf world."[4] Lewis went beyond academic exercises when his wife died and shared his emotions as he traveled from despair to acceptance and was able to see pain as a useful tool by God.[5]

Spiritual experiences may be routine as described by Brother Lawrence[6] or spectacular as described by Bill Wilson.[7] The spiritual experience, in each instance, was transformative. William James referred to spiritual transformation as

> Our ordinary alterations of character, as we pass from one of our aims to another, are not commonly called transformations, because each of them is so rapidly succeeded by another in the reverse direction … but whenever one aim grows so stable as to expel definitively its previous rivals from the individual's life, we tend to speak of the phenomenon, and perhaps to wonder at it, as a 'transformation.'[8]

Spiritual distress is common, and although spiritual distress may be viewed as the negative aspect of spiritual transformation, in reality, it is simply part of the continuum of spiritual change. If, however, spiritual distress continues unabated, its negative effects may increase. Then, intervention may be beneficial. For example, a patient may view an illness as punishment from God. The brief question "Why me?" demonstrates a form of spiritual distress that most individuals experience and must work through on their spiritual journey.

Spiritual distress is not the opposite of spiritual transformation; it is part of it.

Patients may also suffer from loss of faith.[9] Most individuals experience temporary distress, but only a small percentage develop an obsession with such issues. Higher levels of spiritual distress have been identified with poorer health outcomes.[10] Spiritual distress can be measured,[11] and a Spiritual Transformation Scale has been developed that assess both spiritual growth and spiritual decline.[12]

The use of patient narratives has been reported to actually benefit spiritual growth.[13] Patients who have told their stories had added significance to their lives knowing they will help others. Similarly, the lives of patients and others reading these stories will be transformed so that they can realize that their lives can have meaning and purpose. I continue to benefit from the patient-physician relationship, fostered in an atmosphere of compassion along with technology.

Suffering is universal. Much of the civilized world spends considerable time, energy, and resources avoiding suffering. Yet to no avail. At best, suffering is only delayed. There are no quick fixes. Suffering is a process, sometimes a drawn-out process, and it occurs at a price. Often, we experience hope and/or encouragement due to the fact that there is an end result to suffering.

Our response to suffering is crucial. If suffering is unavoidable, then we need to make the best of it. That is, to suffer successfully.

> It is possible to learn to
> suffer successfully.

These stories describe successful suffering. Such an experience is within the grasp of most of us. Although knowing this does not alleviate the suffering, it does facilitate the process.

The Whole World Came
to a Complete Stop

Two-year-old Austin had a "normal" life. He went to day care and played outside with his older brother. But when his parents, Allison and Aaron, found out he had acute lymphoblastic leukemia or ALL, in a few hours, cancer redefined his "normal" life. From carefree times playing with toys and being an active child to countless hours with doctors and nurses, and visits to hospitals and clinics, Austin has battled cancer well. After almost three years of chemotherapy, he remains in remission. This is Austin's story. His mother, Allison, tells how the whole world came to a complete stop—and started up again.

ACUTE LYMPHOBLASTIC LEUKEMIA[14]

Austin was two and one-half years old when diagnosed with acute lymphoblastic leukemia (ALL), a cancer derived from a type of white blood cells known as lymphocytes. Normally lymphocytes live in the bone marrow, lymph nodes, spleen, and blood stream, and help the body fight infection and disease. In acute lymphoblastic leukemia, the most common type of leukemia in children, the lymphocytes divide uncontrollably. Austin's symptoms developed in a period of only a few days and were similar to those of the majority of children and include tiredness, weakness, lethargy, fever, bruising, bleeding, and/or abnormal laboratory results. The spleen and lymph nodes may also be enlarged, and patients frequently have joint or bone pain.

The treatment for ALL is chemotherapy. The first phase of chemotherapy is called induction chemotherapy. Austin underwent almost seven weeks of induction treatment. The treatments are very intense. The powerful chemotherapy medicines require the patient to be hospitalized. Side effects are very common, and Austin suffered many of them.

The second phase of chemotherapy, known as consolidation therapy, was started after a bone marrow exam confirmed that the leukemia cells had been destroyed. The medicines further reduce the number of leukemia cells in the body. Austin received several months of consolidation treatment, followed by three years of maintenance chemotherapy. He received chemotherapy every week during this time. Consolidation chemotherapy attempts to totally eliminate any leukemia cells from the body, but is not as intense as induction or consolidation treatment.

Austin was hospitalized thirty-two times during his treatment. It has been over a year since Austin's last chemotherapy, and he is enjoying time away from doctors and hospitals.

AUSTIN'S STORY

Austin's story is told by his mother, Allison.

My little boy, Austin, loves tractors and has a rubber ducky named "Quack-Quack." At age two, he was diagnosed with acute lymphoblastic leukemia (ALL). His little teddy bear, "Teddy," though now beginning to look a little worn, has been with him all the way.

Almost four years ago, a worker at our day care called and said, "Austin is running a low-grade fever." My husband and I had noticed that Austin looked pale and had begun losing his appetite. He had complained of aching too. When the day care worker called, my husband and I thought Austin probably had the flu. We called our pediatrician for an appointment, and when we got there, Austin's temperature had spiked to 104.7°F.

I started to worry that something other than the flu was going on. Of course, our pediatrician immediately performed blood work. In a few minutes, the doctor came back into the room and told us our son had leukemia. "Leukemia?" we questioned with screaming voices. We were horrified.

> The horror of hearing the word "cancer" or "leukemia" is almost more than the soul can bear.

Our kids are our heroes because they are able to take the day that is unimaginable to most adults and come out with a smile. As a parent, we often have a gut feeling when something is wrong. The longer we waited for the test results, the greater my worry. I felt totally helpless. When our doctor came in and told us that our little boy had leukemia, everything stopped. The noises around us stopped. Outside in the hallway, the whole world came to a complete stop. All thoughts, except those related to Austin, stopped. We found it practically impossible to think of anything else.

Then, thoughts started running through my mind so fast, I could not complete one until another one came to mind. Thoughts like: "This is not right." "The doctor is wrong." "They have the tests mixed up." "This can't be happening to Austin." "What are we going to do?" "Will Austin live?" I was terrified because the only thing I knew about leukemia was that a friend of mine in fourth grade had leukemia and did not survive.

But the doctor told us to go home, pack our things, and get ready to take Austin to St. Jude Children's Research Hospital[15] in Memphis. He had contacted the doctors, and we had twenty minutes to get our things together.

I went home hysterical. I kept thinking, "This isn't right." I was scared. It is all a blur now. I can only remember bits and pieces of what happened. My mother-in-law, a breast cancer survivor who is a patient at the cancer center, met us at our house. We were blessed to have her. She was amazing. She knew exactly what we needed. She had our things packed, and she told me, "Allison, normalcy is no longer normal for you. You need to not worry about anything else in the world. Take Austin to the hospital. You take care of him, and we will take care of everything else here." (She and my mom took care of Trey, our other son, who was four at the time.)

The drive to St. Jude Children's Research Hospital in Memphis felt so unreal. I experienced the longest two and one-half hours of my life. I kept looking at Austin. I kept praying: "Please let him be all right." Austin grew sicker by the hour, and by the time we arrived at the hospital, he was like a ghost; he lay there pale white, fatigued, and motionless.

> The action of helping is more
> beneficial than the feeling of
> being helpless.

I felt very helpless. "Is there nothing we can do?" we asked. As parents, we have always felt we should have some sort of control over our children's lives, especially when they are so young. If they don't feel well, we should help them feel better. If they are having trouble, there is always something we can do. With the leukemia, we could not help. Austin's condition rapidly deteriorated, and we had no time to do anything except get him to the hospital. There was nothing else we could do. We held his hand and prayed.

Austin's disease-fighting white blood cells were essentially gone. He had almost no platelets, and he was severely anemic. When they put the intravenous line in his arm, the small blood vessels throughout his arm and face popped because he had no platelets. I felt so helpless, watching and unable to do anything.

But I did not feel hopeless. At that moment, we prayed to God that our child was in the right hands. We put complete trust in perfect strangers. Our prayers gave strength to our hope, and our hope eventually took the place of the feeling of helplessness.

> Even when feeling helpless,
> we can feel hopeful.

Just a few days before this, we were a normal family. Our boys were playing. My husband and I were making plans for a summer vacation.

Now, as I watched my little boy get sicker and sicker, and all the activity around him from the healthcare providers, I knew the test was not wrong. Austin really had leukemia. This was really happening to us. This was happening to Austin. I cried silently: "What are we in for?" "Can Austin survive the ordeal?" "What about his brother?" So many questions filled our minds, questions that no one could answer. We would have to wait for those answers.

The doctors performed bone marrow exams and started antibiotics. We waited for the results. "How bad is the leukemia?" "What are his chances of survival?" "Did I really want to know?" Thoughts were going through my mind faster than I had ever imagined. They were random thoughts that did not stay on one subject very long.

We were dazed. We would walk through the hall and not even realize where we were. We encountered hundreds of children with different types of leukemia, and cancer was all around us. We were overwhelmed. Within two days, twenty doctors came in and talked to us, examined Austin, and performed tests. Sometimes I remembered what the tests were for, and sometimes I could not remember. They had to place a venous access device (called a central line, port-a-cath, or port) in his chest area, and that required minor surgery. Protocols were brought in for us to sign since we were to participate in a clinical trial. We had to give our consent for his chemotherapy to start. I don't even recall what I read.

But I will never forget our third day. My husband finally talked me into leaving the hospital. I did not want to leave Austin's side because I did not know what was going to happen next. If something bad happened, I wanted to be there for him. But that morning, I left. A nine-year-old boy in a wheelchair got into the elevator with me. He said to me, "Your child was just diagnosed with cancer, right?"

I just looked at him and said, "How do you know that?"

He said, "Well, you have that look." Then he told me his diagnosis and proceeded to tell me about all the chemotherapies Austin would have to take and how long his treatment would probably be, but not to worry because Austin had the best kind of cancer and he was going to be okay because he was in a good place.

This encounter broke my heart. A nine-year-old should never have to know that stuff. A nine-year-old should know when baseball starts. Children should not have to worry about big, real-life problems. They should be having fun.

Children with cancer learn too much too fast. This young boy practically talked like a doctor. At that point, I realized everything I had taken for granted in the past, such as going grocery shopping, walking in the park, or watching a movie. We had to learn to live day by day, sometimes moment by moment; otherwise we could have not coped with Austin's treatments.

> It is important to learn to live one day at a time, even one moment at a time, when facing uncertainty.

Austin went to surgery for his central line and his bone marrow test. The results finally came back and indicated that the characteristics of his leukemia put him at a lower risk of relapse and a higher chance of staying in remission if he went into remission. We learned that just a few years ago, any kind of leukemia would have a poor cure rate, but because of all the research, low-risk patients have up to a 95–98 percent cure rate, thanks to the wonderful work at St. Jude Children's Research Hospital and other institutions.

Austin started chemotherapy. He had lots of side effects: nausea, vomiting, headaches, and even near convulsions. We found it very difficult to watch him be so sick, knowing it was necessary if he had any chance of surviving at all. Side effects cannot be predicted all the time, and we did not know what to expect next.

My husband stayed with me as long as he could, but he had to return to work. It was a hard time for our family. The stress is so intense and prolonged, and the workers at St. Jude Children's Research Hospital told us that there is almost a 75 percent incidence of divorce when there is childhood cancer within a family. My husband and I dealt with the sickness differently. We allowed each other to deal with it in our own way. We decided to allow Austin's sickness to bring us closer together rather than pull us farther apart.

> Parents need to accept that each will handle a crisis differently, and to allow that to happen. Parents can be brought closer.

Our faith was central to our success. It brought us closer together. We realized we should never take for granted the times we had together as a family. Before Austin was diagnosed with ALL, my husband used to go off and do his thing. I worked all the time. The boys stayed in day care. I look back and think, "Why?" We never know what is going to happen in life, and we need to spend as much time as we can making good memories that will last. Our family is now closer. We try to spend as much time together as possible. We want to make wonderful memories.

Material things don't matter as much. We realized "keeping up with the Joneses philosophy" is not as important as what we had in front of us: our children, our family, our health, and our friends. Eighteen days after he started chemotherapy, the doctors delivered the wonderful news that Austin was in remission. I know why it is called intensive chemotherapy. It was tough on Austin. And it was tough on us watching what Austin had to go through. Today, he still takes chemotherapy once a week, and he will continue for several more months. He has been on weekly chemotherapy treatments for almost three years.

When Austin was born, he had a cranial nerve disorder. From twelve months of age until he was diagnosed with leukemia, he saw a therapist who worked on his speech. Austin's leukemia treatment complicated that problem. His first round of chemotherapy weakened his nerves so badly that he lost his ability to speak and walk. A nerve specialist told us Austin would never be at a normal level of walking or talking. The doctor said he would always function at a two-year-old level. But when we went back for a checkup a few months later, Austin amazed the doctor. He said he was wrong. Austin is a miracle baby. Austin runs and plays. He loves to play with his tractor. His grandfather, whom he calls "papa," is a cotton farmer, and Austin loves to see the big tractor in the field. He even goes with his papa to pick cotton. He pays attention to what is around him more than a year ago. When we go back tto St. Jude Children's Research Hospital, he likes to help the other patients and tries to get things for them. He is starting to ask questions, too.

All Austin needed was to be a normal little boy. But he understands more now. I honestly don't think I could have handled it as well as Austin. Trey needed to be a normal boy, too. Now, we have redefined what is normal. We have weekly chemotherapy trips to the cancer center. This is normal for us today.

There were moments where I was resentful toward God and felt angry. A lot of issues surfaced during this time. I am a stronger Christian now. There were moments when I took the Bible and read and read and read, trying to understand. But there is no way to understand, no answer to why God allows illness in an innocent child.

> We cannot understand why illness is allowed in an innocent child. That is an unanswerable question.

I believe it's okay to have negative feelings. You are not supposed to be a rock. Even a rock crumbles when enough pressure is put on it. I have wondered, knowing what I know now, if I would have done anything differently. I have had my share of "what ifs." "What if I had …?" But I have learned that you do the best you can do at that time. You cannot rely on "what ifs."

The doctors and nurses at the cancer clinic and those at St. Jude Children's Research Hospital became our family. They were our sign of hope. There were many days when we did not think we could go on another day. But when we thought we were at the end of our rope and there was nothing else in the world that we could do, our healthcare family came through. They helped us tie a knot and hang on.

Living one day at a time is our new "normal" life. It's a pretty good way to live, but it has been a bittersweet lesson for our family.

THE GIFT OF LIVING ONE DAY AT A TIME

"We learned to live day by day, sometimes moment by moment." Allison's statement offers an effective solution, for not just cancer, but any seemingly overwhelming circumstance or experience. Individuals with cancer and/or their families often arrive at a point where they can make a similar statement. Allison and her family realized that by dwelling on the "normal" past to where they wished to return, or by thinking of the overpowering, insurmountable future, they were robbing themselves of the gift of today. When a relatively simple statement like Allison's is internalized into a lifestyle of daily living, it becomes one of the most powerful means of experiencing life to the fullest.

> The philosophy of living one day at a time is an effective solution to living life to its maximum.

Austin's story made me ask: "How much of each day do I experience?" "Am I living in the 'now,' or am I preoccupied with the past and/or the future?" Initially, when we are facing a life-threatening situation, we spend considerable time living in the past or future because we fear losing the present. And that is exactly what happens. When the precious time of the present is used to regret the past (which cannot be changed) or to be anxious about the future (which may not be), the experience of the present is lost. The desire to be truly alive in the present and the reality of living in the past or future frequently produces a state of tension. The present, past, and future simultaneously occupy parts of our mind and emotional framework. This tension within us, of believing one way and living another, frequently prepares us to be teachable. Allison and her family learned the value of spending time in the present. Much of enjoying life is about living one day at a time. I am thankful for this gift bestowed by countless cancer patients, who have taught me without realizing it.

Living "one day at a time" has proven an effective means of dealing with traumatic or life-threatening events. The phrase largely developed and became popularized through twelve-step recovery programs.

However, its usefulness does not depend on a particular traumatic experience, socioeconomic status, educational level, or intelligence. The lifestyle of "living one day at a time" depends on the willingness of the individual to decide to make the best out of a bad situation. Cancer patients and their families are no exceptions. The "one day at a time" lifestyle works regardless of the source of one's pain, agony, despair, loneliness, fear, anxiety, or hopelessness.

Often, we may ask, "That all sounds good, but what does living day by day, or moment by moment, mean?" First, let's examine what it is not. Living one day at a time does not change the circumstances. The traumatic event remains. Daily living does not ignore the past or not plan for the future. The past remains part of who we are today and helps determine how we respond. Likewise, who we are today determines the future.

For that reason, the past is static. The future is undetermined. Our response to both should be dynamic. Daily living does not avoid the pain and suffering, but faces and deals with it. The past's fear, sadness, and grief must be experienced, for it contributes to our emotional well-being in the present. Experiencing the past allows us to heal.

The ability to live one day at a time is not an automatic response. It does not just happen. And such a lifestyle may actually evade us if we seek it aggressively. The ability to live one day at a time is a by-product of experiencing life events, rather than pursuing it as a goal.

If we do not automatically respond to a distressing event with daily living, how do we learn to experience each day? It is interesting that the quote "one day at a time" is probably derived from a reference to the incurable nature of alcoholism. "What we really have is a daily reprieve contingent on the maintenance of our spiritual condition. Every day is a day when we must carry the vision of God's will into all of our activities."[16] This statement provides us with the solution to the problem (daily removal from what controls us) and the source of the solution (to maintain a healthy spiritual condition). A healthy spiritual condition involves a relationship with God, such that he provides us the strength to do his will. Therefore, daily living is intentional. We make a decision to do it. We ask God's help to live daily. In a way, living one day at a time may be viewed as living in God's presence while surrounded by the reality of life.

> Daily living is intentional if we are to live it to the fullest.

Patients and families have taught me some practical steps to receiving the gift of living one day at a time. The first step involves an awareness of our lack of ability to experience the present in its fullest. As soon as we become aware that it is better to live in the present, we begin actively receiving the gift. Such awareness is not easily accepted. It is part of

Steps to living one day at a time:
1. Awareness of its benefit
2. Focus on the moment
3. Experience thankfulness
4. Redefine normal in the context of reality
5. Celebrate the good of each day

everyone's spiritual journey but occurs at different points along our spiritual paths. When we realize that life is about today, an intentional aspect of seeking the present occurs.

As children, we fully use our ability to live in the present. However, as we age, we lose the ability. We replace it with regrets of the past and anticipation of future events. The present, for many adults, is often a temporary jumping-off place as one moves from past to future and back. Children readily experience the moment. Watch children. They discover each moment. They live in awe rather than in regret or anticipation. Adults have learned how to physically function in the present while they emotionally and mentally live in the past or future. Furthermore, adults habituate to this way of living and become controlled by it.

If awareness that it is better to live in the moment is the first step, the second is learning to think about what we are doing at the moment. We must learn to focus on what is happening exactly at that instance. Is it rubbing our child's arm while he or she receives chemotherapy? Do we feel a soft touch, by a friend, on our shoulder? Do we hear a bird singing on a spring day? Can we feel life as we take a deep breath and slowly exhale? Focusing involves use of the senses—sight, smell, touch, sound, and taste. Try concentrating on one sense at a time. We have learned to "override" being aware of what we sense. We instead think about the many tasks we have to do or those we have not yet completed. The habit of living in the past or future requires, as does any habit, a lot of effort to break. When we find ourselves in "another world," we must stop and refocus. The ability to do this becomes easier. We learn a new way of dealing with life. We learn a new way of living. We start enjoying life, in addition to experiencing it.

After awareness and learning to focus, we learn to be thankful. Our spiritual journey insists that we express this thankfulness. Thankfulness is the third step to the gift of living in the now. We express our thankfulness for experiencing and enjoying life in the present. Even with a tragedy, we may be able to express thankfulness that we can do what we need to do without our minds being anxiously preoccupied. Initially, the ability to live in the now may be short-lived and seem insignificant. Be thankful for that short moment. Progress is measured, not by giant leaps, but frequently by small stumbles. Practice these three steps—i.e., awareness, focusing, and thankfulness—continuously, and you will soon see the results.

As we practice these steps to help us experience the present, whether day by day or moment by moment, we stop attempts to control the future or to live in fear of it. We give up our struggles with the past. Our focus moves from fear, worry, and anxiety toward living in the moment. By living in the present, we maximize the gain and minimize the loss of what we desire—time to live while being alive. As we repeatedly take these steps, we also learn that living in the present requires a redefining of what we once considered "normal." We often think normal is being the absence of suffering, and the presence of all that comprise the good life. As such, normal is an ambiguous term, referring more to an unthreatened well-being. While the absence of suffering may be the desired condition, rarely is it realized for any significant period of time.

> By living in the present, we maximize the gain and minimize the loss of what we desire—time to live while being alive.

The often-heard statement "Just get me through this and back to normal" becomes a diminishing actuality as we realize that normal must be reevaluated and redefined. In reference to our health, our normal life involves keeping thoughts (and hope) on a future of improved well-being, while adjusting to changes in everyday routine. A normal life involves an attitude change. We live, not with the assurance that everything will be all right, but the reassurance that we have the strength to get through the day before us. Some individuals have difficulty adjusting to a new "normal" life because they insist on trying to live the previous "normal" life within the context of the circumstances of the new abnormal life.

Normal may be redefined simply as "what is" each day. The good of each day needs to be celebrated. Normal becomes the life experienced moment by moment. Coping with the diagnosis of cancer will always have difficult moments. Activities that were once enjoyable may be avoided. Laughter may be difficult for some time. When laughing does occur, guilt feelings may arise. A new normal life is constructed around all that must be done. The intensity of the situation with cancer demands much. As the normal life is redefined, life will begin to move forward, often with more meaning and purpose.

Contentment is often a by-product of living here and now, one day at a time. Allison speaks of contentment when she talks of focusing on "What we have in front of us." The apostle Paul, well-known for his suffering, hardships, and pain, as well as his ability to "keep on keeping on," realized he was not content—that is, he was wretched or miserable (Romans 7:15–24)—and years later he wrote that he had learned how to be content (Philippians 4:11–13). What did he do? Paul advises us, as a

> Contentment happens, not as we strive for it, but as a by-product of focusing on what is right at each moment.

practical approach to being content, to think about whatever is "true, honest, just, pure, lovely, of good report, virtue, or praise" (Philippians 4:8–9). In other words, contentment means focusing on the right things every single moment of our spiritual journey. And an improved spiritual condition keeps us moving in the right direction.

Let's enjoy our new normal.

THE SERENITY PRAYER

God, give us grace to accept with serenity
the things that cannot be changed;
courage to change the things that should be changed;
and wisdom to distinguish the one from the other.
Living one day at a time;
Enjoying one moment at a time;
Accepting hardships as the pathway to peace;
Taking, as He did, this sinful world
as it is, not as I would have it;
Trusting that He will make all things right
if I surrender to His Will;
That I may be reasonably happy in this life
and supremely happy with Him
Forever in the next.
Amen.

—Reinhold Niebuhr[17]

My Life Was Surreal; I Could Not Believe I Had Cancer

Annette is one of Dr. Daugherty's first employees. Everyone she sees and has worked with over the last twenty years feels like her extended family. However, her relationship with her employer took on a new meaning in January of 2006 when she was diagnosed with breast cancer. Now, her life is going well, and she loves her job, and firmly believes God put her there.

Early Stage Breast Cancer[18]

Annette was diagnosed with early stage breast cancer. Breast cancer is the most commonly diagnosed cancer in women in the United States and is very treatable, especially when diagnosed early. It is a complex cancer, and while there are standards of treatment, each woman should be treated as a unique individual and the treatment decisions entered into jointly.

Stage I breast cancer refers to invasive (the cancer cells invade neighboring normal tissue) breast cancer in which the tumor is less than two centimeters and in which no lymph nodes are involved.[19] The five-year survival for stage I breast cancer is 98 percent. Cancers have routinely been found at earlier stages since the intense use of mammograms.

Treatment involves some type of surgery, either a lumpectomy or mastectomy, and lymph node evaluation. Annette underwent lumpectomy. In order for a lumpectomy to be as successful as a mastectomy, radiation therapy is required. If Annette had chosen to have a mastectomy, then radiation treatment would not have been necessary.

However, a certain portion of women will have the breast cancer recur after complete surgical removal. The recurrence can be reduced by using adjuvant treatment (adjuvant refers to treatment given in addition to the surgical removal). Annette's breast cancer was small, had not spread to the lymph nodes, and was positive for hormone receptors. After radiation therapy, Annette was placed on an oral medication to block her hormone receptor activity. Adjuvant treatment may include chemotherapy, radiation therapy, and/or hormonal therapy. Premenopausal women may consider removal of their ovaries.

Annette is close to completing her prescribed time on oral drugs. She continues to work at the medical oncology office and advocate for breast cancer patients.

ANNETTE'S STORY

It was just a routine mammogram right before Christmas, 2005. We came home one day and had a message on the answering machine to call "Dolly" at the doctor's office. I found out later that "Dolly" was their code word that something is wrong with a mammogram.

I was told to come in the next day for a spot compression mammogram and ultrasound. I went into overdrive. I left my house and went straight to the oncology office where I work. I was seeing a surgeon that evening. Since it was the holidays, between Christmas and New Year's, everything was closed, and I had to schedule my surgery for early January.

I remember when the surgeon told me I had breast cancer. I was still drowsy from the anesthesia during surgery, but I remember telling him to go ahead and take both breasts off right now. That was my initial reaction, because I worked around this stuff and had seen so much. I wanted to get it over with, all at once.

My sister-in-law was at the foot of the bed shaking her head and saying, "No, no, you need to be calm." It was just surreal. I could not believe I had cancer.

My daughter was a senior in high school, and my son was at UNA (University of North Alabama). We had told all the family that the surgery was not a big deal. It was just a biopsy. My parents did not even come from Huntsville, because we did not think it was going to mean anything. The area on the mammogram was so little.

Well, here we go. My daughter was so affected; she cried and carried on more than my son did, but I think my son just holds stuff in. Both of them were very concerned and worried.

When a loved one is diagnosed with cancer, it is very important that everyone "feels his or her feelings." Emotional honesty is essential during these difficult times.

My husband is a very sensitive man, and he cried too. My family later told me that when I came back from the surgery, my husband, Tony, was there but we did not make eye contact, which was probably a good thing. I think if I had, his face would have told me that I was facing breast cancer. I did not know that the surgeon had already told my family that it was malignant, and he had done a lumpectomy.

I truly believe that if I had looked in Tony's eyes, he would have lost it, because he lost it when we got home. I told him, "Do not do this to me. We have got to do this together, and you have got to be strong." It was the unknown, and he did not know if he was going to lose his wife. Since I worked at the cancer center, I talked to the physicians continuously through this whole ordeal. From the start, they encouraged me to go to another oncologist

> Relinquishing our fears to the Lord, he gives to us a gift of hope for tomorrow. With this gift we help others release their fears to him. His is truly a gift that keeps on giving.

for a second opinion, simply because they were too close to me and felt that I needed to hear what they were telling me from somebody else.

It took me several days to get an appointment, and that was horrid, waiting and waiting. This meant further delay before I could have any lymph node surgery to make sure the cancer was not there. The physicians felt pretty sure it wasn't, but I still was not going to know until surgery. The lymph nodes ended up clear, and after two more weeks, I started radiation.

Meanwhile, I was working. I think I stayed off a week after I had my lumpectomy. I was stir-crazy. It was nervous energy, and I had to do something. I cleaned every drawer in my house. I could not sit, because I would just squall (uncontrolled crying). I could have very easily curled up and decompensated, but I did not let myself do that, for myself and the kids. If it had not been for my fellow employees, I would have been nuts. They rallied around me and supported me.

I had never been sick. I had never been in the hospital. Never had surgery, or ever been put to sleep. That was probably my worst fear, being put to sleep. I know that sounds silly. For the most part, I did really well until I went to church. There I would just lose it emotionally. My surgery was on Thursday morning, and on Wednesday night, I went to church. All the women in the church stood around me, and everybody prayed for peace and calmness. It was what I needed.

I went into surgery the next day, and I was not nervous. My blood pressure was not high. I mean I was really calm, and I know that the Lord was with me while I was lying on that operating table. I knew that it was going to be okay, whatever the outcome. Of course, I wondered why this had happened to me, but I did not have an answer for that. Who am I not to have experienced this?

In the long run, you look back and you can say through all of this, I have become a better person. I believe I am a better employee and can minister to our patients better. I can tell them, "I know how you feel." I know how these women feel when they lay up on that radiation table.

> Almost any tragedy can be viewed as benefit producing. This is not to say that the tragedy happened for that purpose, but that because of the tragedy you can see growth.

I have not had chemo, so I don't know what it is like to lose my hair and some other things, but I have encouraged women who, like me, just didn't know what to do. I have been around a lot of patients, and my having cancer has brought me closer to them at the offices where I work. I feel like I have been able to help some women around here.

I also think I am more outgoing, more approachable, I guess. I say things that need to be said, and a lot of things just don't bother me like they used to. I guess some stuff doesn't matter anymore. I appreciate things that I didn't before.

Some people ask me, "How can you work here?" Even before I had cancer, I liked it. It is what I do. It is my "whatever." With me having cancer, the experience has made me a stronger person, and I am now able to help these people here. I think the Lord has been in this, and it has changed me. I don't know if anybody around here has noticed, but I say it has.

I think my relationship at home is better, not that it was bad. It is just now enhanced, very much so. My husband and I value each other more. He was there for me, cried with me, and held me when I felt bad. Even if I had to have a mastectomy, our relationship would not have changed. I know it would not have mattered to him.

> The benefit produced by cancer extends beyond self and allows the patient to frequently experience improvement in several areas, such as family, work, church, and friends.

My advice to others is you have to learn to let someone else help take care of you. People brought me meals, money to go out for food, fruit baskets, and plants. It is hard to be a recipient of all that, but you just have to let people do that for you. Take care of yourself, and let other people try to take care of you, too. It's okay to be a little selfish during that time.

I started working for Dr. Daugherty part-time in 1987. I was his very first lab technician, and I worked for about a year until my second child was born. I quit work for a while, until she started kindergarten and then went back to work for him. I am still here. This is like family.

Recently, I told my husband I feel like this is where I need to be right now. I am able. I can work more, and I look forward to coming to work. I feel good.

The Gift of a New Perspective

Annette's statement, "And in the long run, I look back and I can say, through all of this, I have become a better person," clearly reflects a new perspective on life and living. More than being a different person because of cancer, Annette developed a vision, or mission statement, for her life. Her passion for living has intensified.

Her vision involves sharing her story with those similarly diagnosed, telling how she became a better person, and helping them along their journey. Annette's journey has become her testimony of faith. Her ministry is defined by what she has learned through her own struggle with breast cancer, as she meets the needs of others as they are diagnosed and undergo treatment for breast cancer. She can honestly say, "I know how you feel." The words are well received. She has walked in the proverbial moccasins of the patient. And as she shares her story, she represents encouragement. Annette is definitely a better person, not necessarily materially or morally, but with a more meaningful and purpose-filled life.

> Our trials and tribulations often define our area of ministry; that activity adding meaning and purpose to our lives.

Let us look at Annette's story. She described the experience as "surreal." Other patients have described, upon hearing the diagnosis of cancer, life as a bad dream, a huge shock, or like the world were falling apart. Statements such as "When will this horrible time end?" "I just want to wake up and discover it isn't true," "This can't be happening to me," are common. Then, one day, as the darkness of night surrenders to the first rays of sunshine, many awaken with a new perspective. That morning may take one fretful night, or it may occur after a thousand. But regardless of how long it takes, a new changed person awakens. A new creature emerges, and the horrible nightmare of having cancer is transformed into the reality of survival. New opportunities arise that would not have arisen if Annette had not been diagnosed with cancer.

> The nightmare of having cancer is
> transformed into the reality of survival.

Annette can view herself as a better person. To view self as "better" indicates some acceptance of not only what has been, but also the response to the past. The ultimate acceptance is saying "I would not have it any other way. I am so changed for the better that I would go through it again just to be who I am today." Not everyone can express such a statement. The reason some experience a dramatic change in thinking and others do not remains a mystery.

Transformation may occur as a quantum change but usually occurs as a process of small changes interspersed with periods of regression.[20] The apostle Paul defined transformation as resulting from a renewing of the mind (Romans 12:1–2). Such a renewing of the mind occurs more easily with some than with others. Our personalities, our life experiences, our responses to those life experiences, the encouraging stories of others, and relationships, including one's relationship with God, all play a part. Paul admonished us to live our lives with a passion toward God's purpose (Colossians 3:23–24). Such also reflects a renewal of the mind. We move from selfish to selfless.

This passion may take the form of a sense of urgency that often accompanies the new perspective of being a better person. Not an urgency to do more things or obtain more stuff, but an urgency to make sure that each "thing" has meaning and purpose.

> The diagnosis of cancer may result in a
> sense of urgency to live with
> meaning and purpose.

Attempting to live each day to its fullest provides significance to our lives. The urgency of living meaningfully is manifest in different ways. Some help others struggling with cancer. Some connect with nature by watching a spider spin a web or ducks float lazily on a pond. Some sit in awe of a sunset or a child sleeping. Awareness of our senses increases. Patients will often make statements like "I thought I couldn't stop and smell the roses before I was diagnosed with cancer, but I am now able to enjoy each day one moment at a time." The minutes, hours, and days are more precious, and there is less wasting time on the unimportant. The new perspective Annette describes involves trust. It is not trust that life will turn out the way she wants it to, but rather trust in God's word that assures good can come from bad in the life of a believer (Romans 8:28).

Trust is a choice—the choice that allows one to "let go" and stop attempting to control. Like Annette, patients will say, "I knew it was going to be okay, whatever the outcome." Such words reflect a spiritual experience, or at least a step along the spiritual journey. They clearly demonstrate a spiritual relationship. Patients who say such are assured that, no matter what happens to them, it is okay because they know where they will live forever.

A changed perspective involves not only trust, but gratitude. Cancer patients are often grateful about just being alive each morning. The apostle Paul describes a joy in suffering because of the results it produces (Romans 5:1–5). Paul is not implying that we are to be happy about the situation or circumstances causing suffering, but that when suffering happens, we can have the gratitude that we can come out of it a better person. James expresses a similar view (James 1:2–6). So gratitude, while an aspect of perspective, is itself a gift and will be discussed in detail later.

Being selfish, in a good way, is an often-overlooked product of cancer. How many times have we been taught that we are to think of others and not ourselves? Patients, however, soon learn the importance of taking care of self. Many start exercising or watching their weight more closely. Many stop smoking. Alcohol consumption frequently decreases. Being selfish can be difficult for some people, especially those who are nurturing and/or caregivers. It may be difficult to stop being a caregiver. Remember what we learned from Allison in the previous story—"learn to live one day at a time, sometimes one moment at a time." We are not giving up nurturing others forever. But just for today, we are taking care of ourselves. By taking care of ourselves today, we are preparing ourselves for service tomorrow.

The new perspective experienced by Annette integrates faith into all aspects of life. And work is no exception. We are interested in our purpose on earth, as evidenced from the best-selling book entitled *The Purpose Driven Life*. God, in contrast to humankind, does not distinguish our work from our ministry.

> Steps to a changed perspective:
> 1. Trust
> 2. Gratitude
> 3. Taking care of self
> 4. Integration of faith in all life's areas

Work is simply the vehicle through which we accomplish our ministry.

We often divide our lives into what is sacred and what is secular. Annette doesn't see it that way at all. She is able to see what some would view as secular (her employment) being congruent with what is sacred (ministering to others). Both are service to God. Work allows a way to manifest love and compassion for humankind. Both are central to ministry. Pope John Paul II wrote, "Awareness that man's work is a participation in God's activity ought to permeate ... the most ordinary of everyday activities."[21] Annette now perceives work as one avenue whereby her life has meaning and purpose. Work can thus be both a form of worship of God and a place of service to fellow humans. Pope John Paul went on to say, "Just as human activity proceeds from man, so it is ordered toward man. For when a man works, he not only alters things and society, he develops himself as well ... This kind of growth is of greater value than any external riches which can be garnered."[22]

Not all patients see themselves as better people. Cancer's impact takes many forms. One breast cancer patient suggested two alternatives:[23] we can become bitter or we can become better. Sometimes, a little bitterness may be healthy as one copes with having cancer. However, when we become trapped in the emotional state of prolonged bitterness, the cancer extends from the body to the spirit. Some bitterness or anger may be directed at ourselves for the lifestyle that resulted in the cancer.

> Prolonged bitterness extends the cancer from the body to the soul.

Bitterness may also be a way to grieve what was lost. Most patients experience some bitterness, especially early on, and this is an opportune time for Annette and others to assist the patient in coping. Bitterness, when left unattended, is like acid, slowly eating away our spirit and preventing us from experiencing and enjoying self from a new wondrous perspective.

Taking a journey, in the shoes of another, produces a new perspective.

What Cancer Cannot Do

It cannot cripple love,
It cannot shatter hope,
It cannot corrode faith,
It cannot eat away peace,
It cannot destroy confidence,
It cannot kill friendship,
It cannot shut out memories,
It cannot silence courage,
It cannot invade the soul,
It cannot steal eternal life,
It cannot quench the spirit.

—Author unknown

While cancer does sometimes do these things, it doesn't have to get control over you. [24]

A Need for Answers

Kenneth has been in the recycling business almost fifty years. Once in a while, he thinks about retiring, saying, his "poor body is worn out on the inside." But he also says his urgent need to understand his situation led him to the spiritual transformation that changed his life. He has survived metastatic colon cancer and now battles metastatic prostate cancer.

Dual Cancers (Colon and Prostate)

It is unusual, but increasingly common, to see people with dual malignancies. The major reason seems to involve increased survival rates for the first cancer diagnosed. This results in an increased chance for a second malignancy, especially if the two types of cancer are related. Ken has battled colon cancer and prostate cancer, as well as a subdural hematoma. He was diagnosed with metastatic colon cancer seventeen years ago. Long-term survival was rare and continues to be, but Ken responded to the standard chemotherapy. He underwent chemotherapy for almost three years because he tolerated the treatments, and each time he was scanned, the tumor continued to shrink. He was cancer-free for about six years.

Ken began having neck pain, and the initial radiological studies were normal. The pain persisted, and repeat studies showed a metastatic lesion in his neck vertebrae. The mass was also compressing his spinal cord. Subsequently, a bone scan revealed many metastatic lesions. He was then diagnosed with cancer metastatic to the bone. He was started on radiation therapy for pain control. The evaluation revealed the metastatic cancer to be from his prostate. His PSA (prostate-specific antigen) was over 3,000. He was started on an antihormone injection as well as a biphosphate compound to improve his bone structure. That was five years ago. He has received radiation therapy on two occasions and has been on chemotherapy since his prostate cancer became hormone refractory three years ago. He is on his fourth regimen of chemotherapy.

Ken and one of the authors (JPD) had the opportunity to go with a group to Honduras and participate in medical missions a few months ago. Ken's story provided hope to countless individuals regardless of the nature of their trial.

KEN'S STORY

My experience with doctors, hospitals, and procedures began twenty years ago. I had a blood clot on my brain. The doctor removed it. He told me the next day, for everything he knew, I should be dead. I told him I am lucky, and he did a good job.

The first day I was diagnosed with cancer, it did not bother me. I had gone in to see my primary care physician for a routine examination, and I had no symptoms at all. I was fifty-three years old when he recommended a screening flexible sigmoidoscopy. Did I get a surprise? A mass was found in my colon. That was Friday. I went to work Saturday to complete some projects so I left nothing incomplete.

While I was working, I called my brother and my two sisters and told them I was scheduled for a colonoscopy on Monday. The reality of it began sinking in. I guess I was too naïve to know all the dangers of what I was about to go through.

I thought, "Well, the surgeon is good." He had told me that, depending on what he found, he would line me up with an oncologist, if need be. It has been seventeen years since I was diagnosed with colon cancer. At the time of surgery, the cancer had already spread to my liver, and they said it would be touch and go. I wasn't given much hope at that time.

I started on chemotherapy, and every time my doctors did a scan, the cancer had decreased in size a few more millimeters. I underwent almost four years of chemotherapy, and eventually the cancer became undetectable on the scans.

My daughter and son were both over the age of twenty at the time of my diagnosis of colon cancer. My kids did not say much. None of us ever say much. But I could tell on their faces that they were very concerned.

However, the diagnosis of metastatic colon cancer did bring us closer. If I am an hour off my routine, my kids start calling, and inquiring: "Where are you?" "What are you doing?" My daughter lives in South Carolina now, and she still calls to check up on me. Sometimes she calls one of my close friends to inquire how I am doing. My daughter does not think I tell her the whole truth.

I do tell her as best I know because there is no need to make anything up. I mean, if the doctor does not tell me, I cannot tell her.

There are so many unknowns when dealing with cancer; I don't try to guess all the possibilities anymore.

I stayed off chemotherapy for several years. About six years ago, everything was going well, when I fell and hurt my neck. The pain kept getting worse. My family doctor put me on anti-inflammatory medicines and even long-acting narcotics, so I walked around all goofy. And the pain was getting worse. I saw a neurosurgeon who told me I had a protruding disk and I needed surgery. I thought, "I'd better see another doctor, but the only appointment I could get was three months away."

The pain became so bad. It got to where my only relief was lying on the floor in one position. I was in the office one day lying on the floor, when the office manager stepped over me and very politely asked for my doctor's number. Of course, I could never get him on the phone, but she did, and he told her to take me to the emergency room.

Shortly thereafter, I was diagnosed with prostate cancer that had moved to the bones. When they put dye in my veins, I knew what they were looking for. Sure enough, I had a tumor between the first and second vertebra. It was big, and an aggressive program of radiation treatments was recommended in an attempt to shrink it immediately.

I ended up taking fourteen radiation treatments. I almost fainted when he told me my PSA was 3,000 instead of a normal 0 to 4 or 5. I thought, "Oh man, I have screwed up now."

Then, when I came back a week later, they told me there were tumors in six different places in my body in the bone.

Not a good report. I thought I had sold the farm; I really did.

My PSA would go down during my treatments and then up again. I thought, "This is like a bomb ticking."

I finally had radiation along with medication and then chemotherapy. I remember telling the doctor, "We can't let my PSA go any higher." There is a limit, and something is going to have to give one day. That was almost three years ago. After about twenty weeks of chemotherapy, the phone finally rang, and the doctor said my PSA had decreased by half.

I hung up the phone, and the tears started rolling. You cannot believe the stress that left me.

During the recurrence of prostate cancer, I went back to church, about three years ago, after being gone for twenty-six years, not attending or participating in any way. I wasn't out running wild. I just did not go.

God was still watching over me, keeping me pointed in the direction he had planned for me.

> A diagnosis of cancer often results in a spiritual realignment with an urgency to increase meaning and purpose.

One day, I got up from behind my desk, shut my door, and sat down to bow my head and pray. Then I started remembering different things about my treatments. I started remembering the first time I started chemotherapy, when I would go to the doctor's office and see people with the same kind of cancer I had, taking the same treatment, but they would fail and die. Yet, here I was, getting along. I thought, "Why them and not me? What is there about me that is able to overcome all this? Maybe it is not about me."

I thought, "There is only one reason for this. God does not want me to die, but this is not a freebie. He wants me to do something, and I don't know what it is." I thought about it a long time, and since I was managing the treatments as well as anybody else, I started calling on terminal cancer patients. I would try to bring them comfort. I don't know how many I called on. I was a pallbearer for a lot of them.

Something else significant happened in my life when I was taking treatment for my colon cancer. A friend at work shared her faith with me. She and I spent many lunch breaks reading our Bibles, talking about what we read, and trying to get a better understanding. I will always believe God introduced me to her as part of his plan. My friend had a granddaughter born during this time, about sixteen years ago.

I took my chemotherapy treatments for colon cancer on Mondays and just felt terrible. I tried to work the afternoon of my treatment, and felt sick on Tuesday, Wednesday, and Thursday. Sometimes, I felt bad on Friday and Saturday.

I became involved in the life of my friend's granddaughter. My friend and I volunteered to babysit every weekend. How I managed to do that, I will never know, but I willed myself to feel good enough to do it. I got to see this little one learn to talk and walk and grow. It was a miracle of new birth to me. I held her and rocked her when she was tired or not feeling well. I fed her. I bounced her on my knee and made her laugh. She was a joy to be around. I carried her when she was tired and couldn't walk anymore. I used to take her for walks and pick her up and show her a bird nest, and she would want to smell all the flowers on the bushes. I would explain how all the birds live in the trees, and she just loved it all. We sat with her every weekend for three years until she was old enough to go to day care.

Then five years ago, the little girl came home from school, and they thought she had the stomach virus, but it wasn't. It was appendicitis. Her appendix burst, and she died. She was eleven. So the last time I got to carry her was as a pallbearer. As I stood at the grave site that November day, my heart heavy with grief and my eyes full of tears, I silently asked myself the questions that are as old as man. "Why? What is happening there? This has to be a mistake. How can this be?" But no answers came.

> Life is a sequence of events, often seemingly unrelated, that move us toward a purpose.

So many things happened, and I did not understand them. What it boiled down to was that I needed to find answers. I was not going to blame God for taking her. I did not think that was the way it was. But I couldn't just stop there. I had to find other answers.

My friend had her knee replaced two years later, and was recuperating at her daughter's, so I went down there one Sunday afternoon. But before I left, I went to this rosebush on the side of my house, and on one of the stems was the most beautiful cluster of roses that rosebush had ever put out. So I cut this runner, wrapped it in wet paper, threw it in the back of my car, and took off. I stopped at the cemetery where my little friend is buried, and I put the roses on her grave.

When I started back that night, I started thinking about my little friend and all the people that she had touched in her short life. When it came down to me, I realized that by trying to get better so I could see her on Friday, that, in fact, this

> To live and declare the glory of the Lord, this surely is the plan he has for our lives. (Psalms 118:17)

little girl kept me alive. This was probably the greatest blessing God has ever given me. My search for understanding was really a search for significance. The next Sunday, I went back to church. Can you believe that? During my time away from church, I know many people prayed for me, helped me, and encouraged me. I owe each of these individuals my eternal gratitude. Each, in his or her way, helped keep me alive. My purpose is to help and encourage others that are suffering.

Later that year, my friend and I were going to visit her daughter. I went to the church sanctuary first and then knelt and prayed for God's will. I prayed that he would put the right words in my mouth so I could break this barrier that her daughter had built around herself and remove some of this grief from her.

I told my friend what I was going to do, and she agreed to keep her other granddaughter occupied so I could talk with the daughter. I am not a counselor, and I was scared to death because, if you say the wrong thing, you can just drive them deeper into depression.

The time came, and I started talking with her. I told her I had known her for over twenty years and that I loved her as much as my own daughter, but I couldn't stand to see what this was doing to her. She broke down and started crying. The more she cried, the more she talked. The more she cried, the more I cried, but she vented some of her feelings.

After that, every time we saw each other, we talked. We still do. I think she has told me things she has never told anybody else. But she still holds this guilt that because she is a nurse, she should have diagnosed her daughter's appendicitis. I don't know when her suffering will end. I don't want to bring up grief-filled situations. She is going to have to, and then I will talk to her about it.

I fully believe I will see the little girl again. When God sends someone down to get me when it is my time to go, I hope she is the one.

I have a renewed life with God. I feel myself grow as I regularly worship God and as I turn my cares over to him. I can say, "Thanks, young child, for helping me realize the important meaning of God's love and the plans he has for each of us."

I continue treatment for the metastatic prostate cancer. During the six years since its diagnosis, I have received hormonal therapy, radiation therapy, and several regimens of chemotherapy. I remain fully active.

Apart from still being alive, I have been blessed many times over. I have seen my daughter graduate from college. Three weeks later I escorted her down the aisle where I gave her in marriage. I have been presented with two beautiful grandchildren. My son kept close watch on me through all my illnesses. The rest of my family is very supportive even though we live hundreds of miles apart. The important things in my life changed from materialistic to inner human needs. I now know the peaceful serenity of the countryside just before dawn, the beauty of a sunrise, the smell of rain, the softness of a rose petal, and the warm breath of a soft baby on my cheek.

THE GIFT OF SERVICE TO OTHERS

For many years, Ken has battled cancer and other life-threatening illnesses. He knows his life needs to count, and that is why he can say, "My purpose is to help and encourage others that are suffering." Today, servanthood is an important topic. Many books and articles link service and leadership. However, these often advocate using service to enhance leadership skills rather than fulfilling life's purpose by serving without expecting anything in return.

Leadership, in both sacred and secular environments, all too often involves manipulating others into doing what we think they should be doing. The gift of helping others transcends this type of leadership through its selflessness. Service becomes a ministry rather than a means of management. The benefit Ken receives from his service

> Service to others without expecting anything in return improves our meaningfulness in life.

is the product of his service rather than the motivation for his service. Service to others is not "benefit dependent."

Many organizations are founded on service, from the 4-H club ("hands to greater service") to Rotary International ("service above self"). Members of such organizations learn the meaning of doing a deed without expecting one in return. Mother Teresa, probably the best known example of servanthood in our time, said "the fruit of love is service; the fruit of service is peace."[25] She viewed a vow of service to the poor as the embodiment of Christ.[26] Yet she, as do many of us, doubted. Her doubt may have provided the basis for her ministry in that through her times of darkness she could better see into the darkened lives of the poor.[27]

Suffering and service are linked. Those suffering (or those with a need) are a means for service by others (or those who will provide a need). A personal history of suffering increases awareness of the need to be of service. While suffering is the great equalizer of need, service is the great equalizer of opportunity.

Ken has experienced suffering. By transcending the circumstances, Ken makes use of his situation to help those who are suffering more than he. When I threw myself a "pity party" as a child, my mother would often remark, "Look around you, son, and see those less fortunate than you." I eventually internalized that message.

The interplay of suffering and service is love. Jesus, often known as the "Suffering Servant," personified the role of love. One result of suffering is that regardless of the cause, it often produces a different fellowship with God. If the extent of the relationship is redemptive, one feels a need to share that fellowship by loving others. The suffering of others is the ideal moment to express that love.

Let's examine the link between suffering and service. When we are having a "normal" life, we don't ask, "Why is this happening?" But when illness and tragedy happen, we almost always ask that question. We often ask because we assume that life is unfair.

Certain personality types "need" information. Ken, having an analytic mind, describes his "need" to know. The reasoning is "If I understood this, I could accept it easier."

> The fairness of life is its
> unfairness.

Perhaps we need to recall the words spoken in *The Princess Bride*, "Where is it written that life is fair?" Could it be that the fairness of life is its unfairness? How many times have we considered ourselves lucky when we deserved punishment or scolding, but did not receive it?

Ken wanted to know why this was happening to him. The dominance of self causes one to ask, "Why me?" Harold Kushner asked the same question and eventually concluded God is not all-powerful, as described in his well-known book *When Bad Things Happen to Good People*.[28] Billy Graham, in his address to the Episcopal National Cathedral delivered September 14, 2001, addressed the question of why God allows suffering and tragedy: "I have to confess that I really do not know the answer totally, even to my satisfaction. I have to accept by faith that God is sovereign, and He's a God of love and mercy and compassion in the midst of suffering."[29]

Suffering is part of life. It is often more so for some than others. Not a day goes by that we cannot see tragedy and suffering, often self-imposed, by those who apparently have all resources available to them.

We are blessed with technology and medicines that alleviate pain, and we want to live our lives without pain and discomfort. Perhaps we seek a state of total comfort. We want to feel good all the time.

However, life screams at us otherwise. Many great writers have told stories of suffering and concluded that suffering is necessary for awareness. Solzhenitsyn[30] says, "Bless you, prison, for having been in my life!" Mother Teresa[31] remarks, "One must really have suffered oneself to help others."

Other great leaders have observed the relationship between suffering, service, and submission to God. Dietrick Bonhoeffer wrote, "The only profitable relationship to others—and especially to our weaker brethren—is one of love, and that means the will to hold fellowship with them. God himself did not despise humanity, but became man for men's sake."[32] In one of his sermons, Martin Luther King, Jr., stated, "Recognizing the necessity for suffering I have tried to make of it a virtue ... I have lived these last few years with the conviction that unearned suffering is redemptive."[33]

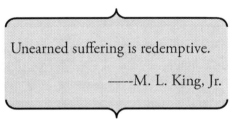

Unearned suffering is redemptive.

——M. L. King, Jr.

In response to a question about what we need to bring into our relationship with Jesus, Brennan Manning[34] said, "Childlike surrender and trust, I believe, is the defining spirit of authentic discipleship." He went on to reply, in response to a question about how to know if one is really trusting Jesus, to say, "The dominant characteristic of an authentic spiritual life is the gratitude that flows from trust—not only for all the gifts that I receive from God, but gratitude for all the suffering. Because in that purifying experience, suffering has often been the shortest path to intimacy with God." Intimacy with God produces Godlike traits in us—the ability to love the unlovable, the ability to serve without expecting in return, the ability to see benefit in suffering. It is also service to others.

On a more modern note, in his sermons, John Claypool, who preached about his daughter's diagnosis and eventual death from leukemia, could eventually say, "If we are willing, the experience of grief can deepen and widen our ability to participate in life. We can become more grateful for the gifts we have been given, more open-handed in our handling of the events of life, more sensitive to the whole mysteries of life, and more trusting in our adventure with God."[35] In the film *Shadowlands*, C. S. Lewis concludes, "Why love if losing hurts so much? I have no answers any more. Only the life I have lived. Twice in that life I've been given the choice: as a boy and as a man. The boy chose safety, the man chose suffering. The pain now is part of the happiness then. That's the deal."[36]

Biblically, suffering is presented as universal, continuous, and benefit producing. Suffering has two aspects. One is the actual suffering or problems, and the second is our response to that problem. In the context of Romans 12:2 and the examples referred to previously, suffering may be viewed as a catalyst for renewing the mind. The natural response to disease and pain is anger, denial, resentment, blame, and a subsequent pity party. A spiritual response is acceptance of what has happened as having value in defining purpose. Ken's story reflects the renewing of the mind. It reflects his moving from being conformed to the world to being transformed and overcoming the world.

As Christians, we have a perfect example of the link between suffering and service. Jesus, God's Son, responded to suffering by praying. He learned obedience, acceptance, and submission from what he suffered (Hebrews 5:7–9). We are to follow his pattern (1 Peter 2:21). Christians can rejoice in suffering because we know the result (Roman 5:3–5). Christians also share in his glory (Romans 8:16–17) and fellowship (Philippians 3:10–11) when they suffer. A case for the necessity of suffering can be made in that suffering has a strong likelihood of enhancing our intimacy with our Creator.

Often, it is only after suffering that we can understand and accept not asking the question "Why me?" In striving for comfort, we may be blind to the way God uses suffering in our lives. Contemporary society finds it difficult to accept suffering as a tool in the hands of a merciful God. We are intolerant to discomfort.

Ken was eventually able to ask another question: "Now that this has happened to me, what do I do?" Ken's search for answers about his disease led him to find answers about himself. The search for "Why me?" led Ken to an understanding that his life was really about service to others. It was time for him to take action and do something worthwhile for those still suffering, perhaps a little more than he was.

One's realization of "doing something for God" often comes about, not in some miraculous manifestation of lights, sounds, or experiences, but in the mundane experiences of everyday life. Ken, for example, simply realized he was still alive. From there, he came to believe that he needed to do something worthwhile with his life, which he viewed as a gift from God. Realization that our area of ministry results from our suffering facilitates our expression of gratitude. If life is a sequence of events, often seemingly unrelated, that moves us toward a purpose, then life can be viewed as a process of discoveries that are a prerequisite to our spiritual formation and subsequent area of ministry.

When we realize that our lives should "count," there is a temptation to either look beyond where we are (anticipation) or to regret where we have been (anxiety). Is it missions in Africa with HIV patients? Working with the homeless? Or is it in our own backyard? Ken took the latter approach. He knew where he was in life. He needed to continue chemotherapy. He had to cancel plans for a mission trip to Central America. But he saw hurting and disadvantaged people all around him when he came to the clinic for treatment. His fellow strugglers were his mission field. Ken bloomed where he was planted. Ken had been, or was, where they were. He could be a source of encouragement. Perhaps he could help them to have a more positive attitude. He could do this daily. Ken identified his area of ministry. The great commission may often be the great omission as the uttermost parts of the world are emphasized over the innermost parts of our community.

We have a purpose on earth. Not necessarily a specific activity, but a series of activities that will give meaning and purpose to our lives depending on where we are on our spiritual journey and by the circumstances and events we face. It is as if we are born with a need to be significant in this world. While many of us search for significance in activities and possessions, when a life-threatening illness comes our way, what is significant is often redefined. When we have meaning and purpose in our lives, the activities of living become more important than how long life is.

To some, suffering of any kind, in and of itself, is meaningless. To others, suffering has meaning by the way we respond to it. If we know the why of our existence, we can bear almost anything.

> Meaningless suffering becomes
> meaningful by the way we
> respond to it.

Victor Frankl[37] maintains we discover this meaning in life in three ways. First, by doing some worthy deed. Second, by value (experiencing something or loving someone). Third, by our attitude toward unavoidable suffering. He states, "What man actually needs is not a tensionless state but rather the striving and struggling for some goal worthy of him. What he needs is not the discharge of tension at any cost, but the call of a potential meaning waiting to be fulfilled by him." Victor Frankl should know, an Austrian neurologist and psychiatrist who survived the Holocaust and detailed his experiences at a concentration camp in a book entitled *Man's Search for Meaning*.

Ken's own suffering did not hinder his expression of love. If anything, it augmented it. Ken had right behavior rather than right circumstances. He acted rightly about his circumstances. Service to others has its origin in love for others. Love for others often has its origin through common suffering. Our love for others comes from awareness of God's love for us, for them, and the connection we have with them as God's children. Service is an action resulting from an attitude.

The attitude of Jesus on service is best described in Philippians 2:5–8. An act of service, either by Jesus or by Ken, is more easily done if one has dealt with the injustices of the past and experienced fresh fellowship with God after his cleansing. John 13:15 is an example. Jesus is the example and tells his disciples

Steps to the gift of servanthood:
1. Selflessness
2. Viewpoint of service being a ministry
3. Independence of benefit to self
4. Love of others
5. Gratitude in the midst of what is happening

he has a new commandment. Actually, it is not a commandment as much as a way of life (verse 35). From now on, the world will know you, not by the keeping of commandments, but by the expression of love. The keeping of commandments often goes unnoticed by an unbelieving world, but the action of love is always noticed.

> Our words often go unnoticed.
> Yet the action of love is noticed by
> the unbelieving.

Jesus tells his disciples that there is hope for the future. They will be reunited. It is time to show love and not anger. We have our future assured. What can we do but serve God by serving others. The emphasis is not on what God can do for me, but what I can do for others as I show God's love. It is about past forgiveness and future assurance. With these taken care of, it is all about now.

Rick Warren, in his book entitled *The Purpose Driven Life*, states that we are shaped to serve God. Every time we serve others, we are serving God. We may live a very short life or a very long life. That is usually not our choice. It is what we do with our lives that is our choice. Service to God through service to others requires compassion, especially for those less fortunate than us. Compassionate service has several enemies, such as self-centeredness, striving for vocational success, and busyness. When the diagnosis of cancer enters one's life, priorities change. While we remain selfish in wanting to live as long as we can, we sometimes experience a remarkable transformation, and self-centeredness all but disappears. I once heard Dr. Hans Selye, after being asked how to live a stress-free life, remark, "Earn your neighbor's love."[38] Service is how we demonstrate our love, expecting nothing in return. I have learned, like Ken, that now is the time to live a life of service in spite of suffering, circumstances, or problems.

A willingness to serve lessens the need to have answers to unanswerable questions.

Success

He has achieved success
who has lived well,
laughed often, and loved much;
who has enjoyed the trust of pure women,
the respect of intelligent men
and the love of little children;
who has filled his niche and accomplished his task;
who has left the world better than he found it
whether by an improved poppy,
a perfect poem, or a rescued soul;
who has never lacked appreciation of Earth's beauty
or failed to express it;
who has always looked for the best in others
and given them the best he had;
whose life was an inspiration;
whose memory a benediction.

—Bessie Anderson Stanley, 1904[39]

I Turned It Over to God

Almost eight years ago, Maudie, a great-grandmother, was diagnosed with multiple inoperable brain tumors. The brain tumors were metastatic cancer from her lungs. She underwent chemotherapy and radiation treatments, and Maudie became what medical science calls a "miracle."

Metastatic Lung Cancer with Brain Metastasis

Stage IV lung cancer has a poor prognosis. Maudie presented to the hospital with the lung cancer already metastatic to the brain. That was eight years ago. Maudie experienced symptoms of dizziness, loss of balance, double vision, syncope, and blurred vision for a few weeks before she came to the emergency room. A CT scan showed multiple metastatic lesions on both sides of her brain. A CT of the chest showed a 4 x 3 cm mass in the left lung. A bone scan showed lesions in the sternum and thoracic spine. She also had an enlarged lymph node in her neck. A sample of the lymph node was removed and found to be a type of lung cancer that had spread to the lymph node. She was started on steroids to reduce the swelling in the brain. She was treated with radiation therapy to the brain. She responded well.

As soon as Maudie completed her radiation therapy, since she responded so well, she was started on chemotherapy. She received weekly chemotherapy for a total of thirty weeks. An evaluation at this time revealed complete resolution of the brain metastasis, improvement in the bone scan, and shrinkage of the primary lesion to 2.5 cm, and resolution of the lymph nodes. She was becoming fatigued by this time, and the decision was made to give her a break and chemotherapy was stopped. However, within eight months, the cancer in the chest was growing. Since a PET scan revealed this to be the only disease, she was started on a new chemotherapy regimen and received six months of weekly treatment. She reached maximum benefit from the chemotherapy, and since she had residual tumor in the mediastinum, she underwent radiation therapy.

Maudie completed that five years ago and remains without any evidence of cancer. She continues to take care of her grandchildren and to be active in church.

Maudie's Story

I have been living in north Alabama since about 1945. I was about two years old. When my father got out of the army, we came to live with my grandmother and step-grandfather. I have a daughter, two grandchildren, and two great-grandchildren.

Almost eight years ago, I was in the grocery store arguing with the cashier that I had already paid him.

He said, "No, ma'am, you did not."

And I said, "Oh, yes, I did." My friend who was with me had already taken her groceries to the car. Since it was taking me so long, she came back in to see what was wrong.

I told her, "Would you please get me out of here?" I do remember that much. It was around that time that I was feeling a bit down some days, and I just kept forgetting things. I moved to a new place, and after I moved there, I could hear this noise.

I would wake up at night, and it was like a drum beating in my head. As it progressed, it kept getting louder and louder. Then, I started hearing the noise during the day. My vision started getting blurry. I was just so weak.

I told my doctor that I was hearing these things, and she said that I just wanted to get "high." My doctor was teasing with me, just playing around. I would tell my daughter, "It sounds like someone is beating a drum!"

So my doctor gave me some kind of pill. I was just completely out of it. One day, my grandson and another lady had to carry me to the car. They took me to my doctor, and she said she didn't know what was wrong, but would find somebody who could help. She admitted me to the hospital. They started doing tests as soon as I was admitted. The doctors from the cancer clinic were asked to see me.

When the results of the tests came back, the doctors told me I had a brain tumor. Actually I had multiple brain tumors. They could not be removed surgically. They also told me that the tumors started in my lung.

My pastor came in and said, "How can you lay up here and be so calm? Do you understand what they said?"

I told him, "Yes." I said, "You know what I did, Reverend? I turned it over to God. I'm just grateful to be alive."

My daughters and family were all crying and going on. My pastor said that when he came by, they would all be out there carrying on. Then he would come in to see me, and I would just be lying there smiling. I said, "Well, there was nothing I could do."

In the beginning, our family doctor told my daughter she wanted to talk to her outside the examination room. All at once, my daughter came back and said, "Come on, Momma, we are going." She told the doctor, "God is not ready to take my momma from me yet." The doctor wanted to call in hospice because the prognosis was so grim.

Then, when I went to the cancer clinic, everybody, even the infusion nurses, said they all just looked at each other and wondered about me receiving treatment. I was in a wheelchair, but they started working on me, and look at me now.

I don't know what the next go-around will be, but I can tell the world about this. I just thank God.

> Gratitude is a precious commodity and is related to overall quality of life and to spiritual transformation.

I remember times when I would go to the doctor and not really know I was there. I lost my memory, which was expected from brain tumors. My daughter had the doctors' numbers on pads of paper in each room at my house. But I never gave up.

I have never asked God "Why me?" I asked him, "Why am I still here?" I talk to him like I am talking to you. I am not complaining and not ready to leave here yet.

I said, "There were so many of my classmates, church members, and friends that were coming to see about me, and they are dead and gone." My pastor has said that God is leaving me here for a purpose.

I get a little depressed now and then, but most days I am up. I pray the same every day and just wait it out. I just turn it over and let God do whatever he wants to do.

When I was taking chemotherapy and radiation at the same time, I got sick and vomited one Sunday. That was the only time. My throat got really irritated from the radiation. It felt like I had swallowed a pin when I tried to swallow. I did lose all my hair, but it finally grew back.

I have grown more humble. You have to humble yourself to him. Before all of this, I was not really talking to God like I should.

God is blessing me and keeps me going. I tell people to have faith in God.

The doctors refer to me as their "miracle patient." They say I have defied all medical and scientific knowledge, and I am not supposed to be here. I am supposed to be dead. The doctors have been so kind to me. It is so important, when you don't feel well, to have doctors that just don't push you through, but give you a little time. I thank God for my cancer doctors and my radiation doctor. There were times when I didn't remember going there.

> True miracles are from the hands of God. He alone can accomplish a miracle with the problem we place in his hands.

Not long ago, my grandson came in and said that my pastor was talking about me. The pastor's wife had cancer, and the pastor said, "We can beat this. Maudie beat seven tumors, and I know that we can beat one."

Have faith in God. Talk to him and pray. Don't wait until something bad like cancer happens. Turn it over to the Master, to God. Go to church, give your tithes, and give of your time.

THE GIFT OF SURRENDER

Maudie, in response to her pastor questioning her calmness, remarked, "You know what I did, Reverend? I turned it over to God." Typically, we react to bad news with resisting hands rather than surrendering ones. Many people, including followers of God, have difficulty understanding or accepting Maudie's statement. Expressions like Maudie's are often made by an individual who has learned through previous adversity that God cares for his children in difficult times. In contrast, if we lack the experience of God caring for us, as is often the case with our more affluent society, we do not appreciate what it means to "turn it over to God."

> When we react to bad news with surrendering hands, rather than clinched fists, we are often teachable.

Maudie felt gratitude to be alive rather than grumpiness about the circumstances. Some people take days or months to come to grips with the diagnosis of cancer. Others, like Maudie, take a matter of minutes to hours. Statements such as Maudie's are founded upon acceptance of what a person cannot change, surrender of the circumstances to one able to change them, regardless of whether they are changed, and gratitude simply for being alive.

> Choose gratitude rather than grumpiness.

Many people cannot immediately turn a problem over to God. A good place to begin is John 16:33 (KJV): "These things I have spoken unto you, that in me ye might have peace. In the world ye shall have tribulation: but be of good cheer; I have overcome the world." Many will pray to God to show them how to overcome the problems and trials of everyday living in order to "be of good cheer." God's Word gives us an opportunity to see how this is done. In Romans 5:3–5, we are told that our problems produce perseverance, character, and hope. Our problems help us to internalize Proverbs 3:5-6 (KJV): "Trust in the Lord with all your heart, and lean not on your own understanding; in all your ways acknowledge him, and he shall direct your paths."

Yet I know many people who have a strong walk with God who have difficulty letting go of that over which they have no control. Though not easy, many people successfully turn it over to God and let God keep it. The ability to "let go and let God" also depends on our personalities, background, and circumstances. As with most matters in life, practice helps, and one can be encouraged by beginning to practice with small things.

Maudie's attitude, seemingly a paradox, is to "surrender to win." Usually, we view surrender as a sign of defeat. But by being "defeated of self," we become more open to surrendering to God. In the case of defeat, we must surrender against our own will. Surrender is difficult.

Surrender was difficult for Jesus as demonstrated by his prayer in the garden of Gethsemane. Jesus, the mortal human, cried out, "Oh, my Father, if it be possible, let this cup pass from me; nevertheless not as I will, but as you will" (Matthew 26:39, NASV). "Now is my soul troubled, and what shall I say? 'Father, save me from this hour'? But for this cause I came into this hour" (John 12:27, KJV). Jesus' prayer indicates surrender of self. Jesus is willing to surrender. He conformed his will to the will of his Father. When we reach the point of surrender and we are willing to let God be in control, then we find life (Matthew 16:25).

It is time to be practical. How do we surrender like Maudie? First, surrender does not mean giving up hope for victory, although frequently used as such in reference to battles. Surrender means letting go of whatever keeps us from the fullest possible dependence on God.

Second, surrender is a choice. We must make a decision to change. Made in the image of God, we are decision makers. Making a decision implies change in approach or direction, and a change in our positional relationship with

> Steps to the gift of surrender:
> 1. Let go of what is preventing dependence on God
> 2. It is a choice requiring action
> 3. Self-examination is necessary
> 4. It is voluntarily commitment to one's belief system
> 5. Purposeful gratitude

God. Our journey moves us from being in control to being in submission. Our journey moves us from calling the shots to seeking the guidance of the Holy Spirit. Our journey moves us from knowing it all to being teachable.

However, a choice by itself does not accomplish what is needed. The decision must be accompanied by action. The first action is making the decision anew each day. Maudie makes a daily decision to turn her will and life over to God. In our will, the battle to control occurs. The battle must be won daily by surrendering to God.[40]

Third, self-examination is necessary. Look for those instances when surrender happened in your life. Not in the keeping of commands and doctrine necessarily, but in those instances when you did not have to be in charge, instances in which you showed love to the unlovable, patience to those demanding, and serenity when not being in control. A few examples of surrender set the foundation for a life of surrender.

Is it not strange that we want to surrender to God, but usually cannot do that unless God helps us? Jesus prayed for help. We can talk to God and ask his help. If you are not used to talking to God, or do not know how, you might consider the following, which has worked for millions of people who needed to surrender their will and life to God. "God, I offer myself to you—to build me and do with me as you will. Relieve me of the bondage of self, that I may better do your will. Take away my difficulties, that victory over them may bear witness to those I would help of your power, your love, and The Way of life. May I do your will always?"[41] Memorize the prayer. Say it over and over. Make it a part of your daily routine.

Fourth, surrender is voluntary. Let us look at surrender a little differently. When we choose to surrender our will and life to God, we do so voluntarily and willingly as part of a belief system that is also the source of meaning and purpose in our lives. In a way, surrender occurs when we decide to be bound to another, in this case, God. Surrender is really commitment. We become committed to a life lived to honor God. Just as individual success in the secular world strongly relates to commitment, spiritual success works similarly. Surrender precedes action, and action indicates commitment. Commitment involves consistent adherence to one's belief system. Maudie is committed to her continued dependence on God. She practices this daily, and she enjoys spiritual success.

Fifth, surrender, in addition to commitment, requires an element of gratitude. Gratitude may be impossible if we view God as the cause of cancer. Disease and illness do not routinely originate from God. Our responses of gratitude to these products of humankind's rebellion to God, however, do originate from God. Gratitude can be a powerful coping strategy, whether you have been diagnosed with cancer or not, and the ability to be thankful benefits our health. Cancer patients are often more grateful than the population as a whole.[42]

Purposeful gratitude is the way to start the day and the way to end the day. In between these two events, a natural outflow of gratitude will more likely occur. We live in a complaining world. Gratitude goes against the grain of this earth. However, gratitude is, as Cicero stated, "not only the greatest of virtues, but the parent of all the others."

An "attitude of gratitude" produces positive emotions, and positive emotions aid in coping. Studies have shown that gratitude actually enhances production of chemicals that help our immunity and healing systems.[43] If we are positive in our thoughts, we will attract positive people and, thus, enhance, though our connectedness, further positive emotions.

Albert Schweitzer said, "To educate yourself for the feeling of gratitude means to take nothing for granted, but to always seek out and value the kind that will stand behind the action. Nothing that is done for you is a matter of course. Everything originates in a will for the good, which is directed at you. Train yourself never to put off the word or action for the expression of gratitude." Expressing the heart of the matter are words by Alfred Painter: "Saying thank you is more than good manners. It is good spirituality."

Melodie Beattie writes, "Gratitude unlocks the fullness of life. It turns what we have into enough, and more. It turns denial into acceptance, chaos into order, confusion into clarity ... It turns problems into gifts, failures into success, the unexpected into perfect timing, and mistakes into important events. Gratitude makes sense of our past, brings peace for today and creates a vision for tomorrow."

> Gratitude unlocks the
> fullness of life.
> —M. Beattie.

When we realize the importance of acceptance and gratitude, the realization comes with humility. Humility can be described as "being teachable." It is a virtue. In our culture, humility cannot occur without decreasing our egos, a great difficulty for some. The equality of each member of the human race was demonstrated when Jesus washed the disciples feet. Humility allows one to ask, "Why not me?"

Perhaps Maudie could so easily turn it over to God because she practiced these virtues daily. Try it and see if it works for you.

LIFE IS AN OPPORTUNITY

"Life is an opportunity, benefit from it.
Life is beauty, admire it.
Life is bliss, taste it.
Life is a dream, realize it.
Life is a challenge, meet it.
Life is a duty, complete it.
Life is a game, play it.
Life is a promise, fulfill it.
Life is sorrow, overcome it.
Life is a song, sing it.
Life is a struggle, accept it. Life is a tragedy, confront it.
Life is an adventure, dare it.
Life is luck, make it.
Life is too precious, do not destroy it.
Life is life, fight for it."

—Mother Teresa

Worry about Nothing; Pray about Everything

Pam, a retired schoolteacher, has a passion for teaching little children. She worked with Head Start for many years, and eventually taught computer and special education classes. Fifteen years ago, her life changed. She was diagnosed with cancer, and now, she believes she is God's miracle who has been delivered from the "snare of the trapper of the deadly pestilence, cancer."

HEAD AND NECK CANCER

Squamous cell carcinoma of the head and neck (SCCHN) is rare in a young, white, nonsmoking, nondrinking female. Pam was shocked at the diagnosis. She was a mother, Head Start teacher, and children's minister. She had ten-year-old twins at home.

She was having headaches and had been diagnosed with Bell's palsy a few months earlier. Now she had an enlarging mass below her lower jaw. Biopsy showed it to be metastatic squamous cell carcinoma. Her workup was negative for cancer. On direct laryngoscopy, she was found to have a small (1 cm) primary tumor on the right base of the tongue.

Pam underwent radiation therapy to her neck area, with a boost to the base of the tongue. During her radiation therapy, she underwent chemotherapy with the intent of shrinking the tumor prior to surgery. The use of chemotherapy serves to kill cancer cells directly and to sensitize them to the radiation therapy. After radiation and chemotherapy, she underwent a radical neck dissection on the right side. During her treatments and following surgery, she was unable to eat and had to be hospitalized several times. She received nutrition through an intravenous line.

Ten years later, she experienced progressive painful swallowing with a significant weight loss. One year prior to that, Pam had blockage of her carotid artery on the right side, and a stent was placed in order to keep the blood flowing. These problems were consistent with side effects of radiation therapy. She also experienced some radiation-induced damage to her brain and also experienced seizures.

Pam remains disease-free after seventeen years. Although she has suffered numerous problems secondary to the radiation therapy, she remains optimistic and is an encouragement to others.

PAM'S STORY

I found a lump behind my ear sixteen years ago, the day after Christmas. I didn't think anything about it. It was just a little place, and I soon forgot about it. It didn't hurt. I was perfectly healthy. Or so I thought. I had been a little tired and had occasional migraine headaches in the weeks preceding the diagnosis.

The mass enlarged. I went to my local internist. After unsuccessful treatment with antibiotics, he referred me to a surgeon for a biopsy of the enlarging mass. The surgeon found about four enlarged nodules, and the biopsy revealed metastatic squamous cell carcinoma of the head and neck. But the physicians couldn't locate the origin of the cancer. No one in my family had ever had cancer. I did not know what to expect. It was overwhelming. I was referred to another surgeon, who specialized in head and neck cancer, in another city. And still, he couldn't find the origin. However, he decided to go ahead and perform a radical neck dissection where he would remove all the cancer and lymph nodes as well as other structures of the head and neck that may be involved with cancer. This surgery, I learned, is performed when the cancer has spread widely throughout the neck.

I was scheduled for surgery. I was in the operating room and was asleep from anesthesia. The surgeon decided to look into my throat area with a light just one more time to see if he could find the point of origin of the cancer. And he found it. The cancer had started on the right side of the base of my tongue. He stopped the surgery.

I woke up alone in the recovery room. There was no family or doctors around. I lay there for about an hour, and I thought, *Well, they didn't do the surgery. The cancer is too far advanced. It's too late, and nothing can be done.* I was becoming a nervous wreck.

Eventually the doctor came in with my family and told us they had found where the cancer originated. They wanted to change the protocol and try radiation and chemotherapy and do surgery later. They told me I had squamous cell carcinoma of the head and neck, and it had spread to my lymph system. I had stage IV head and neck cancer.

That was sixteen years ago. I was forty-two years old with a sixteen-year-old daughter and twin boys who were ten. I was a homemaker, a

Head Start teacher, and children's minister at the church we attended. I was a devoted wife with a devoted husband. Doug was with me all the way.

No one in my family had ever had cancer. I found out that the cancer I had was rare in young women. And usually found in older men with a history of heavy smoking or tobacco use and heavy alcohol consumption. I had never smoked or drank alcohol.

Cancer! It was a terrifying word to me and my family. There is an indescribable feeling that goes with that word. I didn't know what to expect. All was so new. Fear of the unknown caused panic and numbness at the same time. I was shocked. How could this be happening to me?

> A diagnosis of cancer
> disturbs out sense
> of well-being.

I returned to the cancer clinic to begin chemotherapy treatment. The doctor explained the purpose of the treatment and the possible side effects. He said, "We are going to be aggressive in our treatment. You are young, and you can tolerate it." And I said, "Put it to me. I want to live."

Of course, my thoughts continued to be, "Why me?" Everybody is human, and I just couldn't believe it was happening to me. I couldn't believe this little knot had turned into this ordeal and was taking up so much of my life. "Why, God, is this happening?" "I've tried to be a good Christian most of my life." "I have children to raise." "I have a husband to be with." "Why me?" But then, I turned right around and said, "Why not me?"

There was one certainty in my life that I held on to with all my strength. I wanted to live. I wanted to live to see my children grow up, and I wanted to grow older with Doug. So the greatest battle of my life began. I prayed constantly: "Lord, help me through this and be with my family."

If I got up every day and put my clothes on, it was a good sign. I had to get up. My treatments were pretty rough. The combination of radiation and chemotherapy was difficult. I would receive the chemotherapy as an outpatient and then become so sick that I had to be admitted to the hospital. It just did me in. I kept vomiting.[44] I could not eat. All my nutrients and vitamins were given through an intravenous line. The ambulance came to the hospital and took me to radiation. I had to continue the treatments. I kept thinking, "I have to keep on." "The surgery, after the shrinkage with chemotherapy and radiation, would be less disfiguring." "My chances of survival are better if I keep going."

My church family brought us food every day. I couldn't eat, but my family did. I was having medicine and intravenous fluids brought to my house. I had a port. I was having radiation. My husband learned to do all the nursing at our house.

> Drawing strength first from God and then family and friends allows our reservoir of strength to replenish so we can continue to fight.

My children hated seeing me sick. The night before I had to go for a treatment at the hospital, all the kids would just melt down and cry, "Momma, Momma, please don't go."

I would say, "It is okay. It will make me better."

I had valleys, real lows. Side effects from chemotherapy and radiation therapy resulted in my tongue splitting. I could not eat. My cheek and the roof of my mouth were the most sensitive places. I had to be fed through my veins.

But I felt God's presence. He was there. I knew God did not cause the cancer. God allowed it to happen. I have never blamed this on God. Years later, I looked back, and it was like God was saying, "Look what I can do for you. Look what I got you through." I did not have doubts about God. I just felt low. I was so tired and had pressures coming from everywhere. It was a wake-up call, but it put everything into perspective.

> A spiritual lesson learned by most patients centers around becoming more dependent on God.

In the background, if any of my family members thought I was going to die (and I think they did), they never shared that with me or my children. They just did not want me to leave them.

I remember when my hair was coming out, and I had my marks for radiation. I came home, and it was my son's first baseball game, and I said, "Well, here is your momma!"

He said, "You look like an Indian!"

I said, "I can go to your ball game or not."

He said, "I don't care. You look kind of cute. Okay."

Even our pastor announced from the podium that everyone forgot it was Indian day except me. Everybody had a good laugh. I went to church as long as I could. I had a good support group.

I received six months of intensive chemotherapy and almost eight weeks of radiation therapy. For six long months, my family and I went through every emotion one could imagine. There was so much blind faith, especially during the first few weeks. I had so many tests and endured many visits to the doctors I did not know. But God led me through all the terrifying tests. I had guardian angel nurses who were with me through the darkest times.

We experienced many valleys during the treatment time. Our faith in God, my doctors, and family kept me going. My husband is now "Mr. Mom," and I thank God for him daily. Doug learned to care for me, to nurse me, and to take care of the household chores and errands with the children. Doug is such a prayer warrior. Prayer soothed the soul when good news was lacking.

Sometime during these difficult six months, I experienced a moment when I realized all the worrying I was doing was not accomplishing anything I really wanted for my life. At this point, I decided to worry about nothing and pray about everything. This was difficult to do sometimes. But I kept on trying, and eventually it became second nature. As soon as I found myself starting to worry or having a pity party, I started praying. It became easier and easier. "Worry about nothing, pray about everything," became my motto.

> The key to learning a new habit, one that is far more beneficial, is to decide to do it, practice it in light of doing it imperfectly, and do not give up.

When I completed the chemotherapy and radiation treatments, I had a radical neck dissection. After a lot of additional tests and scans, I heard another foreign word—NED (No evidence of disease). I rejoiced at hearing this wonderful-sounding foreign term and praised God for the healing he had bestowed.

And I went on to give testimony of what God had brought me through. So many people have come to me and said that I have blessed them, some I don't even know. They tell me I have been strong. People see me as strong and courageous. I view myself as totally dependent on God. I tell my doctors what an encouragement they are to me.

I had to have checkup doctor visits, scans, and tests. I was always afraid of bad news. However, about two years after my surgery, I finally decided that the fear of cancer was not going to control my life. Even if the cancer did come back, I would fight it, and I knew God would be with me. I have seen my children marry and grandchildren be born.

I have used my faith. I don't know what is going to happen. I may be gone tomorrow, but I live each day the best I can and live it with hope, thinking the best will happen. Things happen and things change. Miracles happen. I try to be as active as I can, especially with family and church. My faith is important to me. Psalm 91 was read to me every night. It was my source of strength throughout the treatment times. My husband or one of our children would read it to me on the days I was too sick to read it myself.

THE GIFT OF NO WORRY

Pam could say, "I realized all the worrying I was doing was not accomplishing anything I really wanted for my life. At this point, I decided to worry about nothing and pray about everything." What did Pam want for her life? She wanted to live. The desire to live is a part of being human.

Our lives are often defined around our attempt to survive. We can make it through a lot of difficulties if we keep a hope in front of us. Often, we talk of living for physical reasons, but the true enjoyment of life comes from spiritual living. Jesus said, "I came that they may have and enjoy life, and have it in abundance, to the full, till it overflows" (John 10:10, AMP). Pam had done everything in her power to have good health and enjoy life, but there remained the uncontrollable element. Accepting this is difficult but necessary for a full enjoyment of life. Pam learned, as many do, that we are powerless over much of what happens in our lives.

Bad things just happen. If we cannot change the circumstances, we are better off to accept them. "Why Me?" is a necessary question to ask.   It is part of the survival process. I see some patients who view this question as a lack of faith. We can be paralyzed by such a question simply because it lacks an answer, other than "Bad things just happen." Pam moved beyond having to answer "Why me?" and started living successfully by enjoying each moment, realizing that by worrying, she was losing precious moments.

> It is important to ask "Why me?" It is often more insightful to ask "Why not me?"

Pam's faith does not tell her "everything will be all right," or that she will live for years. Her faith proclaims that as long as she lives, she will live in hope, believing the best will happen. Her faith helped her realize that worry was not only unproductive, but it was counterproductive. Worry strangles the life from us. If we are to enjoy life to its fullest, worry must be conquered. We spend much of our lives worrying about things that happened in the past. We cannot do anything about past events unless we accept responsibility and attempt restitution. Worrying about future events also occupies a large amount of our time. Most future "worry" events never occur. More than 90 percent of what we worry about never happens. The small amount of worry that does happen we generally have no control over.

So why worry? Much worry centers on the fear that our lives will be shortened or difficult. But when we worry, we do exactly that—take away from enjoyable life and make it into a miserable life. By giving up worry, you gain what you are worrying about losing.

Those who worry should examine Pam's statement and its three components: (1) she realized what she was doing was not beneficial, (2) she made a decision to change, (3) the change had both a negative and a positive component—stop worrying and start praying.

Let's examine each of these components. Such a realization resembles a spiritual awakening. All of a sudden, a

> **Steps to the gift of no worrying:**
> 1. Realize worry is counterproductive
> 2. Accept what you lack control over
> 3. Decide to try to change
> 4. Look for the good in each moment
> 5. Substitute a positive action
> 6. Entertain the possibility of a spiritual component

light goes off at that "aha" moment, a moment when we internalize truths so that we may act upon them. The truth that Pam wanted to live "clicked." She also realized that worrying only took away time she could be living.

Pam made a decision. The decision involved moving from one way of life to another. The old way (worry) had taken its toll on her. Jesus told us in the Sermon on the Mount: "Take therefore no thought for the morrow: for the morrow shall take thought for the things of itself. Sufficient unto the day is the evil thereof" (Matthew 6:34, KJV). Mahatma Gandhi said, "There is nothing that wastes the body like worry, and one who has any faith in God should be ashamed to worry about anything whatsoever."[45] I saw a quote on a church sign once that stayed with me. It read, "Worry is prayer to an unknown god." Dr. Haddon W. Robinson stated, "What worries you masters you."[46] Jesus told us not to worry (Matthew 6:25–34, KJV).

Our relationship with God often influences how we face problems. People of faith need to exercise their faith to the point of responding to life's problems with prayer. You may state: I know people who have a deep faith and who worry. How can that be? It is my experience that the most faithful person I have ever known was lacking in some aspect of his/her spiritual journey. As imperfect people, we will maintain a part of our lives that needs improvement. As imperfect people, the spirituality we practice is one of imperfection.[47]

Paul provides a spiritual connection between worry and prayer in Philippians 4:6: "Do not be anxious about anything, but in everything, by prayer and petition, with thanksgiving, present your requests to God." Pam's familiarity with scripture allowed her to have a positive task to replace the negative one of worry. It was prayer.

Prayer is so much more than what we think of generally, which involves putting our needs before God. How many of us have prayed that God make us more dependent on him, regardless of what it takes? But the stories of cancer patients are filled with examples of how they learned dependence on God. The disease seems to move us from totally self-centered praying to spiritual-centered praying.

There is nothing special about being able to pray. It is just talking with God. But sometimes we have to stop talking and listen to what God is saying. Sometimes the greatest prayers are one word, a cry, "help," or an exclamation, "thanks." Prayer helps us cope with our problems. I do not know how it works. I trust it does. And I know Jesus tells us to pray.

Prayers provide for intimacy with God. Praying is a good time to tell God how we feel. So cry out. We can tell him our anger, frustrations, desires, fears, and joys. Since communing with God requires no magical or special ways except authenticity, we can express it all. God hears our spirit. Praying for others helps us avoid self-centered prayers. Recently I was attending a fifty-eight-year-old man in the intensive care unit of a hospital. He had been diagnosed with advanced lung cancer and required 100 percent oxygen to breathe. Yet he was joyous. As we got to know each other, the subject of God came up, and he pointed to a list on the bulletin board. Someone had provided a list of people for him to pray for. He prayed all day, repeatedly, and kept his mind off his condition. By continuously praying for others, he, like Pam, had no time for worry.

> Praying for others helps prevent self-centeredness and moves us along our spiritual journey.

Jesus addresses the problem of worry in Matthew 6: "Therefore I tell you, do not worry about your life, what you will eat or drink; or about your body, what you will wear. Is not life more important than food, and the body more important than clothes? Look at the birds of the air; they do not sow or reap or store away in barns, and yet your heavenly Father feeds them. Are you not much more valuable than they? Who of you by worrying can add a single hour to his life?"

The next time you start to worry, pray. Perhaps thinking of *The Lion King* will help get you in the right frame of mind by recalling those famous Swahili words, *hakuna matata*. Simba was taught by Timon and Pumbaa to forget his troubled past and think about the present.[48]

Prayer of St. Francis[49]

Lord, make me an instrument of your peace,
Where there is hatred, let me sow love;
where there is injury, pardon;
where there is doubt, faith;
where there is despair, hope;
where there is darkness, light;
where there is sadness, joy;
O Divine Master, grant that I may not so much seek to be consoled as
to console;
to be understood as to understand;
to be loved as to love.
For it is in giving that we receive;
it is in pardoning that we are pardoned;
and it is in dying that we are born to eternal life.

Using the Most Powerful Medicine

As a hospital administrator, Charles spent most of his career in the "cancer business." Back in the mideighties, he recruited Dr. Daugherty as the first medical oncologist to northwest Alabama. He believes the area could not have gotten a better person, both medically and spiritually. In his view, Dr. Daugherty is sensitive and responsive to the needs of his patients, one of which is Charles himself.

Prostate Cancer

Prostate cancer is the most common non-skin cancer in American men. One in six men is diagnosed with prostate cancer. The older you are, the more likely you are to be diagnosed. Sixty percent of the prostate cancers are diagnosed in men older than sixty-five. Charles was surprised to be diagnosed with prostate cancer at his age. Currently different organizations have different recommendations about screening in asymptomatic men for prostate cancer. As in most situations, the decision should be entered into by the patient and the physician, based on current evidence-based medicine. If the prostate cancer is not very aggressive, it is not wise to offer a treatment program that has many complications.

Over ten years ago, he was diagnosed with adenocarcinoma of the prostate after a screening PSA was found to be elevated. He was treated with palladium seed implants at a larger medical center and did extremely well for the next three years. When his PSA increased, he sought advice from a large cancer hospital and he was started on a series of hormone treatments. After about three years, the cancer spread to his bones. He was recommended to begin chemotherapy and a bone-building drug. He continued on chemotherapy for the next two years. Charles eventually had to stop chemotherapy because of persistent suppression of his white blood count and platelets along with marrow infiltration with the prostate cancer. The boney lesions worsened, and his pain increased. He required multiple blood transfusions.

Charles lost his battle to prostate cancer after eleven years. He was able to share his faith with many individuals and frequently expressed his looking forward to be in the presence of God. His last verbalized wish was for his friends to come to faith.

CHARLES'S STORY

I'm a Southern boy, born in Mt. Pleasant, Texas, and grew up on a farm in Mississippi. My mother and daddy were real true solid Christians. Our whole life was centered around family, church, and school. They provided a firm foundation for me.

After I finished high school, my daddy wanted me to get an apartment in town and go to work for the railroad. I didn't want to work for the railroad. I enrolled in the radiology training program at the Baptist hospital and became a radiological technologist.

I loved hospital work and eventually decided to get into hospital administration. I worked at hospitals in Louisiana and Mississippi before coming to Muscle Shoals, Alabama. While administrator at Muscle Shoals, I was responsible for recruiting the first oncologist to the area. Several years later, I moved to Anchorage, Alaska, and then returned to Muscle Shoals after four years.

When I retired from the hospital business, I joined a group that built radiation treatment centers. That was about twelve years ago, and we built another five or six radiation centers. I am now president of that company. Even with the metastatic prostate cancer, I am still working.

Along the way, though, about eleven years ago, I went to my physician just for a checkup and had a screening PSA, which is a blood test for prostate cancer. The PSA was slightly elevated, and he referred me to a urologist who did some additional tests. The ultrasound showed a nodule in the left lobe of my prostate. I had a biopsy of that area and went home to wait.

Marsha, my wife, and I had a large yard, and we worked in it on Fridays. This Friday afternoon, I had come to the porch to sit down for a drink of water when the phone rang. The urologist was on the phone. He said, "Charles, I have the report from the biopsies that were done on your prostate last week, and I found them to be positive for adenocarcinoma in the left lobe." He then said, "I do feel you would be an excellent candidate for surgery at an attempt for a cure." He suggested that Marsha and I come to see him in a couple of days, and we could discuss the options. The Gleason score of my cancer came back as an eight. The higher the value of the Gleason score, the worse the prognosis. Some physicians told me I would live, on the average, about seven years.

They wanted to operate. At the time, we did not do some of the things we do today, so we started searching for the best options. After a lot of prayer and guidance from God, I decided not to have surgery.

> For most of those seeking spiritual guidance, the answer does not come from an audible voice, but from an assurance of making the right decision.

I had a "radiation seed implant" at a large referral hospital. For three years, things went well. Then my PSA started going back up. That was eight years ago.

Being in the "cancer business," I knew a lot. I knew that was not good. I started searching for the best physician, and the best procedure. I asked, "Who is the best person to see?" "Where is the best hospital?" "What should I do?" "I wanted to live."

In the weeks and months that followed, I learned a lot about God's love. I learned that his Word speaks to our every need. Second Corinthians 12:9 (ASV) says, "My grace is sufficient for you, for my strength is made perfect in weakness. Most gladly therefore will I rather glory in my infirmities, that the power of Christ may rest upon me."

> Spirituality is important to the majority of people in America, and the importance increases with health problems.

The results of the evaluation were a real setback in our lives. After talking to several cancer specialists, they told me that the cancer was outside the prostate and microscopically somewhere else in my body. At this point, Marsha and I grew really concerned. But then one day, on the way home from work, a real peace came over me when I was reminded about what Paul said in Philippians 4:13 (KJV): "I can do all things through Christ who strengthens me." I never worried again and just asked God to have his will in my situation. They put me on a strong regiment of medication to suppress the returning, but still unfound, cancer. Often, I felt so helpless even to get through another day. But David wrote in Psalm 138:7 (KJV), "Though I walk in the midst of trouble, thou wilt revive me: thou shalt stretch forth thine hand against the wrath of mine enemies, and thy right hand shall save me." And revive me he did.

At first, I was thinking more about what I could not do. I was concentrating a little too much on worldly things. It took me a few years to really understand that God's Word was the original and most powerful medicine known to man. I sought out the best doctor and hospital and debated what I should do. You know, I looked at all the

> When the complexity of trouble encircles, find the simplicity in the truth that God is in control and rest in his ability to navigate your journey.

worldly treatment options. The answer came to me one day. As I rode along, all of a sudden, I understood. I had been a Christian for a long time, and I had always asked God to have his way in my life. But I was not looking at God's Word for healing.

> Worry is a meditation, so to speak, on what we are losing or what we cannot do. Worry will be countered by meditating on what we have and what we can do.

While you should seek the physician, the healing will come through Jesus Christ, the Savior, and his Father. That is where the real healing comes from. But you know God does not heal everyone.

At the pool of Bethesda, Christ walked up to the man sitting in his bed robe and asked him if he had been in the pool. The man could not get in the pool because it was always full. Jesus told the man to get up and walk and the man was healed (John 5:8-9). He had been sick for thirty-eight years. Jesus saw the man in the temple sometime afterwards and talked with him. The healed man left the temple and told others that Jesus had made him well.

You know, Christ could have healed everyone in the pool that day. He did not. And he may not heal me. If you ask God to have his will in your life, and he heals you, you ought to be really happy about it. But if he does not heal you, you have to be happy about that, too. You have to be just as happy. As Paul says in Philippians 4:11 (KJV), "I have learned in whatsoever state I am, therewith to be content."

I don't want to leave my family and my job, but I do look forward to walking down that street of gold and it being my turn to hold his hand.

> The peace that goes beyond understanding is often associated with a hope of eventually living without suffering.

When Marsha and I were first told that I had cancer, it was scary. It really was. I learned all I could about prostate cancer, and the more I learned, the more questions I had. I thought, "Not me, Lord, I don't have cancer." The word *cancer* is a terrible thing. Absolutely terrible. But I will tell you what it has done. It has been the greatest blessing for bringing our family closer together. It has brought me closer to the Lord. I have different values than I had before being diagnosed with cancer. There are a lot of bad things that happen to people, like car wrecks and divorce, but when you are told you have cancer, you think, "Gee, how long am I going to live?" "Do I get my affairs in order now?" "What do I need to do to provide for my family?"

After three years on the second program of treatment, we had another setback. My PSA again began to rise. The cancer was going to succeed in taking my life. This was my lowest point along this journey. The doctor said, "Charles, I don't know a whole lot more we can do."

"Am I at the end of my road?" I asked.

After a lot of prayer and direction from God, Marsha and I decided to go to another major cancer center. We wanted to make sure we had covered all possibilities. After going through another round of testing, the doctor told us that he would try an old drug, and if that did not work, then I could participate in a series of clinical trials. That gave us hope. He said I had one to three years to live.

But I told him, "That is with God out of the equation. With God in the equation, all things are possible."

It is hard for physicians to tell you your life expectancy. One told me I would not live seven years, and I am working on eleven. At the last center, I was told that I would not live six months. That was more than six months ago. Whatever time I have left, I am to live it to serve God in my best capacity and be the kind of vehicle he would want me to be. I will go out with a wave of glory so to speak. That is, when the time is right.

I felt frightened and sad when I was diagnosed and each time the cancer appeared to be getting worse. It was equally hard for my wife and family. I have had to be really sensitive to that. But we are taking this journey together. At first I focused on worldly things. Now I focus on spiritual matters. My whole family has a peace about it. They are certainly still sad, and it still brings tears to their eyes and mine, too. But when I began to feel bad about the possibility of the cancer squeezing out my life, Marsha was there to comfort me. We have found comfort in 1 Thessalonians 5:11 (NKJV): "Therefore comfort each other and edify one another, just as you also are doing." Marsha and I grew closer because of my situation.

I have asked "Why me?" I think that is just a natural thing. I don't think God caused me to have prostate cancer. When a tornado comes through, he does not direct it. A lot of things just happen. We don't know exactly why. Cancer does not select good people or bad people. It is simply in that gene, or a combination of unknown events, and that is the way it is. Of course, understanding it is so complex today. It seems simple, but it is not. It is just the way it is. Bad things happen to good people, and good things happen to bad people.

I have gone through a lot of treatments, a lot of failures. At my lowest point, I thought I was at the end of the road. They started talking to me about clinical trials, and I knew that I may get the placebo, and that was not something I was willing to do. I have grown spiritually during this experience. It has given me an opportunity to help others as they travel the road of living with cancer. It is important to share our strengths, joys, and hopes. Sharing is a means of healing.

One of the things we discovered in the Psalms is that we not only have a Lord God and a Savior when we face tragedy, we also have a wonderful friend. David expressed his emotions. He poured out his heart to God. Psalm 23 is full of friendship. Isn't it wonderful to think that God, the Creator over all things, is our friend? Isn't it great to know that in the midst of trouble, he hears us? He is always available to guide us in every decision we make.

Every one of the physicians has said that prostate cancer would squeeze my life out. It would take my life. It finally got into my bones, and about a year ago, the scan showed it in my skull, rib cage, spine, and pelvis. I thought that I may not make it very long, but then I am alive three years after it first appeared in my bones. And here I am working on eleven since I was diagnosed. I am certainly not going to give up. I am just not going to let the devil win this.

The best thing to come from this journey with prostate cancer is that I have gotten a lot closer to God. Through that blessing, it is all I want to think about all day long now. Everything we do for him, we get to take with us to heaven. I want to glorify God. I want to witness to other people what God has done in my life. It is such a joy when people tell me they know they will spend eternity with God.

It is important to read God's Word. Ask God to help in making decisions. God hears us. God knows us. God loves us. If we believe in him and the cross, we will one day spend an eternity with him. That assurance brings peace. I pray for God to have his will in my life, and I am willing to accept what happens. My prayer is not that my suffering be removed, but that I can deal with it.

The Gift of Spiritual Transformation

Charles's journey led him to a change. "At first, I was just thinking more about what I could not do. Concentrating a little too much on worldly things. The best thing to come from this journey with prostate cancer is that I have gotten a lot closer to God. Through that blessing, it is all I want to think about all day long now. Everything we do for him, we get to take with us to heaven. I want to glorify God. I want to witness to other people what God has done in my life."

I have known Charles for over twenty years, and I have witnessed this change. He has urgency about his remaining life. He wants to make his time count for God. For many of us, we want to be remembered, not for the success of our secular life, but for the significance of our spiritual life. Work remains important to Charles. However, the reason for working has changed. Charles no longer views work as a means to make of livelihood, but as a means to demonstrate Christ living within him.

Charles made a choice. Initially he was concentrating on what he could not do. He started to think about what he could do. Then he changed and he moved from a secular emphasis on living to a sacred emphasis. Charles no longer desires success (although he has that), but he desires significance (telling people about improving their life by knowing God). The diagnosis of cancer or other tragedies confronts the very dimension of living and predisposes us to an increased awareness of our meaning and purpose in life. As such, spiritual matters are often brought to the forefront. Charles's life demonstrates that a crisis such as cancer can serve as a catalyst for spiritual growth. Suffering can be a catalyst for transformation. In the spiritual transformation study reported recently,[51] two factors were shown as important in the history of those individuals self-identifying as having undergone transformation. These two factors include a history of religious involvement and a history of personal tragedy.

"And be not conformed to this world: but be ye transformed by the renewing of your mind, that ye may prove what is that good, and acceptable, and perfect, will of God" (Romans 12:2, KJV). Focusing on solutions, being content, regardless of circumstances, and living full lives reflect a renewed mind. The characteristics of a renewed mind reflect a spiritual solution rather than a physical solution. One way to renew the mind is by hearing and reading the stories of others who have traveled similar journeys.

Charles, like most patients, prays for a healing. Praying to be healed does not limit God to a physical healing of disease. God wants people to love and follow him, not from fear, but from appreciation of what he has done for them. Fellowship with him is desired above our good health. Healing restores us to the state that God intended. That is, to be in harmony with him. Charles has that healing on earth. But we need to have the same attitude toward God regardless of whether God grants our requests. Our relationship with God cannot be enhanced only when our prayers are answered the way we want. Our attitude toward God eventually evolves from one of expectation of personal benefit to one of anticipation of glorifying him, regardless of what he does for us.

> We often learn to anticipate ways of glorifying God, and that is often how meaning and purpose occurs in our lives. More often than not, it takes place in the context of family and work.

Is this not a healing of the spirit? In Charles's case, the healing occurred, not in removing the prostate cancer, but in his reconciliation to God. At the same time, it must be recalled that Charles lived longer than anyone predicted, and healing, just as indicated in scripture, was always temporary. Charles enjoyed a healing of his spirit that was not temporal; he lived his life.

The theme of transformation is not uncommon in these life stories of individuals with cancer. Yet evidence suggests that positive emotional/spiritual/religious change can come as a result of cancer and that having experienced a positive change predicts better adjustment several years after diagnosis.[52] Spiritual decline was associated with poorer adjustment, and interventions were recommended as a possible consideration for amelioration.[53] Charles's story, itself a type of intervention to improve dealing with cancer, goes beyond coping and aspects of spirituality typically measured in such studies as those referenced above. Charles has undergone what some would consider a quantum shift in his thinking. While the traditional view of scripture

(Romans 12:2) deals with sanctification regarding moral behavior, the transformation described by Charles deals with a more spiritually practical sanctification. The inner perceptions, thoughts, and attitudes of everyday living with a life-threatening illness, namely cancer, primarily constitute Charles's transformation.

Transformation, as described by Paul (Romans 12:1–2), implies an ongoing change in the believer. As such, any event, especially traumatic ones, is simply a catalyst for an enhanced rate of transformation. The usage of the term implies a responsibility from the individual. As a believer, with the Holy Spirit as counselor, the recipient allows the Holy Spirit to be active in their

Steps to the gift of spiritual transformation:

1. A crisis or personal tragedy
2. Relationship with God
3. Willingness to change
4. Emphasis of significance over success
5. Awareness that suffering can be a catalyst for change
6. Surrender of self

lives. In other words, the will of self must surrender and be willing to be changed. How does this happen? It happens through the renewing of the mind. Theologically, the one being changed gives permission to be changed. This is somewhat akin to the saying, "When you are willing to learn, a teacher will appear." Our progressive transformation makes us more like Christ (Philippians 2:5, 2 Corinthians 3:18, Ephesians 4:22–24, and 1 John 3:2).

A mental image equivalent occurs in the biological world with metamorphosis. It is usually easier to equate oneself with the lowly, icky worm, but more difficult to identify with the beautiful monarch flying overhead. The change is not a fluctuating change. It is not a wishy-washy change that depends on the company with whom we find ourselves or the circumstances in which we live. It is a permanent change. The change is a step upward, perhaps small, toward the lofty butterfly. Metamorphosis also causes a different outward appearance (in the form of what is important) and a change in habits.

Paul referenced the outward appearance of Christians, as well. The inward change has already occurred. We are redeemed. Our lifestyles should reflect that redemptive change. Paul tells us this is not a one-time event, like redemption, but a multiplicity of events in sequence to move us toward Christ. Our way of thinking must change to result in transformation. The transformation does not just involve behavior that indicates how good we are (that may change with a different set of circumstances and people). It involves one's spirit in unity with the Spirit of the Creator. It involves a desire to be with God rather than just doing his commands.

> Spiritual change is a continuous event in the life of a child of God as long as the Holy Spirit is given permission to accomplish the renewal.

The potential of the butterfly resides in the worm. When metamorphosis takes place, that which was on the inside is manifest on the outside without reference to what was. Likewise, spiritual transformation is all about the change that takes place allowing the spirit of God residing in his children to be manifest to the world as Christ's likeness. The world sees a different person. God sees a different person. The change describes spiritual reality. What is inside the person? It is not about the outward appearance. This may be why there is so much interest in transformation in the current literature, both sacred and secular.[54, 55] The church has focused on superficiality of behavior, but the world and churched people do not like that focus. That is why Dallas Willard can say, "We must flatly say that one of the greatest contemporary barriers to meaningful spiritual formation in Christlikeness is overconfidence in the spiritual efficacy of 'regular church service,' of whatever kind they may be. Though they are vital, they are not enough. It is that simple."[56]

How is this inner redeemed nature manifested outwardly? It is in our daily living. It involves more than an outward appearance of attendance at a church service. It is where our new redeemed nature shows itself and how we work, play, and interact with others. It is about how Brother Lawrence has been described as enjoying the presence of God.[57] It is the result of that daily battle of the wills when the winner of the daily battle is God. Daily, what God has done on the inside must be made manifest and visible on the outside. The Holy Spirit desires to see Christians change.

Transformation involves the mind. The word "mind" refers to the mind with emphasis on reflective intelligence, and calls it our seat of understanding. It is that part of the human entity that provides us with the ability to think. With our minds, we can perceive situations, analyze data, and interpret emotions. In Romans 12:2, the mind is equivalent to what is typically referred to as the heart.

Charles knows that life is not so much about how long one lives as it is about how well one lives. And that is transformation.

I Am Among Men Most Richly Blessed

I asked God for strength, that I might achieve;
I was made weak, that I might learn to humbly obey.
I asked for health, that I might do greater things;
I was given infirmity, that I might do better things.
I asked for riches, that I might be happy;
I was given poverty, that I might be wise.
I asked for power, that I might have the praise of men;
I was given weakness, that I might feel the need for God
I asked for all things, that I might enjoy life;
I was given life, that I might enjoy all things.
I got nothing that I asked for, but everything I had hoped for.
Almost despite myself, my unspoken prayers were answered.
I am, among all, most richly blessed.

—Unknown Confederate soldier's prayer. This poem is alleged to have been found on the body of a young Confederate soldier from Georgia.

A Feeling of Peace Took Over

Teena was diagnosed with cancer at age twenty-one. Now, at age thirty-seven, she is blessed to have three daughters, a wonderful husband, and a dream career working with cancer patients. She inspires those who know her, and she offers hope each and every day.

Hodgkin's Lymphoma

Hodgkin's lymphoma is also known as Hodgkin's disease. It is a historically important tumor as far as demonstrating the curability of cancer. Hodgkin's disease was one of the first cancers to be cured with radiation therapy, and one in which many of the principles of chemotherapy were demonstrated including the curability of the disease with combination chemotherapy.

Teena was diagnosed when she was twenty-one years of age. She had not been feeling well for several weeks, and a knot started to grow around her collarbone. A biopsy reveal she had nodular sclerosing Hodgkin's lymphoma, and her workup revealed she had stage IIIB disease, that is, disease on both sides of the diaphragm. When patients have a history of fever, night sweats, and weight loss, they are considered to have B symptoms. She underwent combination chemotherapy for seven cycles. She experienced several episodes of low blood counts and required transfusions and treatment with antibiotics. Years later, she developed avascular necrosis of the right hip, secondary to the steroids she received during treatment, and was treated with bone graft.

She remains an active wife, mother, and employee. She has three daughters and works in the medical oncology office where she received her chemotherapy. She remains disease-free after eighteen years. She is a source of encouragement and strength to many patients, and especially her treating physicians.

TEENA'S STORY

I know people hear the word "cancer," and they are scared of it and hate it. I don't know that I can say it is the best thing that ever happened to me, but it sure did make a huge difference in the path I took for the rest of my life and the outlook I have on life now. I mean major. If I had to go through it all again to be where I am today, I would.

I was twenty-one years old when it started. I had flu-like symptoms for a few months and couldn't get over it. I was going to school and working, and I thought maybe I wasn't resting enough. I couldn't figure it out. I was not getting enough sleep, but then, that's all I wanted to do. My roommate and best friend in the whole world, Leslie, kept saying something was wrong with me, and I needed to go to a doctor. Of course, I was stubborn back then. And I was scared. I had never been sick and hadn't been to a doctor since I was five or six.

I kept putting it off. I thought I would get over it and I would be fine.

Finally, my mom made me go to her doctor. At that point, I had a knot in the area of my collarbone. It looked like a golf ball sticking up. The only disease I had ever heard about that involves swelling on your neck was mono, so that's what I thought it was.

This doctor, an older man, had been practicing a long time. I respect him now, but when he told me, "We need to biopsy that," I thought he was crazy. He did no tests, no exam, and no blood work. I looked at my mother and said, "No."

He said, "Yes, we need to do it on Friday." That was a Tuesday.

"No, you're not," I insisted. "I have to work." We started arguing, and the doctor told us to please work it out and let him know.

We left his office, and I told my mother, "That man is not going to touch me. He doesn't know what he is talking about. I have mono. Take me to somebody else."

Well, that night, I started running such a high fever and had such bad chills, it scared my roommate, and she didn't know what to do. We couldn't get the fever to break. She kept telling me she was going to call my mother. I told her if she called her, my mom would take me to the hospital and I didn't want that. My roommate ended up calling her anyway, and off I went to the emergency room. I have apologized so many times for being so stubborn.

After my fever went down, the doctor did a biopsy. When I woke up, he was standing there, and he patted me on the shoulder and told me it was Hodgkin's disease. He asked me if I knew anything about Hodgkin's disease.

Strangely enough, I didn't know what it was until about a week before, when I saw a movie with my mother. I have never been able to find the name of it, but there are two girls with cancer, and one has a good attitude and beats it, but the other one with a poor attitude dies in the end.

Well, somehow, a feeling of peace took over. I did not understand it. I just accepted it.

The doctor told me it was okay to cry. I think my eyes filled up with tears. One tear fell down my cheek, but I told him I did not need to cry because I was going to be okay.

I feel as if God put me in that time and place to watch that movie. He was there with me, telling me, "You are going to be okay, but you have to be strong."

My family fell apart, even the men. I remember them wheeling me back to my room, and I could tell one of my uncles had been crying. You know, men can really stir you up more when they cry. I had always thought he was the toughest man. I didn't want my family to do that. I didn't want to be the reason they were doing that.

My mom was a basket case, and my stepdad was wonderful to me. He had pretty much raised me, and I never saw him cry until then. It was all touching, but I told them they couldn't do that. I told them I couldn't have everybody crying if I am going to be strong and get through it. I said if you have to cry, go home and do it and come back when you're stronger.

I was going to make it.

Then, I met the oncologist. My first step was to have the dreaded bone marrow biopsy. That was not fun.

> The word "cancer" is often whispered. It is one of the most dreaded and feared of diseases. Often, there is an intense crisis. Every dimension of living is confronted by cancer.

Up until a year ago, I did not even realize how serious my disease was.

I had heard about people getting Hodgkin's and only having to go through radiation for several weeks, and I would think, "That is nothing." But I am glad that I didn't know more because it would have scared me more. With the information I had, I could be strong enough to get through it. I did not realize how far along my disease had progressed; my only hope was chemotherapy.

Yet I never felt like I was going to die.

I had seven rounds of chemo some sixteen years ago now. I took some pretty strong, heavy drugs, and my blood counts bottomed out. I had to drop out of school because I could not focus on my studies.

I learned the hard way to be honest with your doctors and not always be so positive. I would lie to myself that I was feeling good. One time, I passed out in the cancer office, right after the doctor told me I would feel better if I had a blood transfusion. I told him I was fine. And then I passed out in the hallway. Of course, he admitted me to the hospital, and I received a blood transfusion. That was probably my lowest point, physically.

The whole experience has made me look at life so differently. It did, because I never knew when it was going to end. Before my illness, I thought I would live forever, and I think people go through life thinking cancer is never going to happen to them.

When I turned thirty, my ex-sister-in-law started giving me a hard time about getting old. She is about six years younger than me. I told her, "I am never going to cry about getting old because when I was twenty-one, I did not know if I would live to see thirty." So I enjoy every birthday. Hodgkin's disease has helped me to live life, and now my kids are the center of my universe.

That I could even have healthy children was a blessing. A possibility existed I might not ever have children. But I took the risk. After I had my second child, I starting having hip problems due to necrosis, and I had a bone graft. They put part of my fibula into my hip bone that was dying. That was seven years ago, and hopefully, that will last my lifetime.

I have an opportunity to go to nursing school and fulfill my earlier dream. I am not saying I will never do it, but I don't want to miss out on any of my kids' activities now.

Since I talked my oncologist into putting me to work, this has become my dream job anyway. I know I could make more money with an RN degree, but money is not what makes you happy. For some reason, I feel this strong need to be here at this clinic right now. I don't know why. I want to be an inspiration to others going through this because it is a tough road, very tough.

> Out of adversity … dreams are birthed.

I also want to be here because I feel like every patient who finds out that I went through something similar gets a little piece of hope. I feel good when patients tell me I am helping them. They know they may not survive, but just to have somebody to relate to who has been there and knows a little about the side effects makes a difference to them.

It bothers me to think of those who don't believe or have faith in God. It hurts, and sometimes I get really emotional. For some reason, I believed I was not going to die, but that if I did, it was God's will and that made it okay. That was the peace I had. Either way, I would be fine. God has his plan for you, although it may not always be the way you want it to be.

We had one emotional patient today. She was crying, saying she didn't think she could go on. I told her, "Yes, you can. We are going to help you and do this together." She said she felt all alone, so I gave her my phone number, and others in the office went to her aide. By the time she left our office, she was smiling and told me she loved me. That's all I need to have a good day's work.

I believe I have found my life path. I still think I have a lot more of that path to cover.

> Cancer can serve as a catalyst for spiritual growth.

The Gift of Inspiring Others

Teena said, "I want to be an inspiration to others going through this because it is a tough road, very tough. I also want to be here because I feel like every patient that finds out that I went through something similar gets a little piece of hope." This is why she can make such a statement as "If I had to go through it all again to be where I am today, I would." She has clear vision of the benefits in her life because of cancer. She is comfortable with what she is to be doing with her life.

What is inspiration? There are multiple definitions. We may read about inspiration in the context of divine influence. That is, inspiration allows for the sacred to be revealed in or through a person. Inspiration may be viewed as a process by which the mind and emotions of an individual are tied to a creative event, such as art, music, or writing. Others think of inspiration as an inner drive causing one to do an act or to be creative. Which of these definitions best apply to Teena's story? There are several aspects of these definitions that apply: (1) relationship with the divine, (2) allowing one's life to be influenced by the divine, (3) a process of improvement, (4) a creative event, and (5) an inner drive.

The movie like Teena and her mom watched together about attitudes brought to mind another movie of attitudes toward situations and cancer. The movie *Stepmom* that was filmed in 1998 with Julia Roberts, Susan Sarandon, and Ed Harris—families pulling together in difficult situations to give hope to the patient and to the patient's family and extended family. A positive attitude with hope is a beautiful thing in real life; it just reinforces one's needs even in the movies.

Teena's relationship with God has only improved since her initial diagnosis and treatment. As her relationship with God improved, she found her life more influenced by sacred than secular desires. Teena's life, although not easy at times, can be seen as a process that has resulted in her being at a point in her life when she would do everything over exactly the same to be who she is today. Inspiration, as used in the context of these narratives, refers to the act or process of influencing another individual.

> Inspiration is about a vision of hope. The hope one has
> experienced becomes tangible to one needing hope.

The events of Teena's life have given her an inner drive. Inspiration is not as much about that "aha" moments of finding a solution to a problem, as it is about a vision of hope. Inspiration, an untouchable and unseen inner drive or spirit, moves the recipient from one place to another, from a place of fear to safety, hopelessness to hopefulness, helplessness to help, anxiety to peace.

What is the source for inspiration? Clearly, as in Teena's case, it can be a traumatic event like being diagnosed with cancer. According to Robert Kennedy, "Tragedy is a tool for the living to gain wisdom, not a guide by which to live."[58] In this context, inspiration is simply sharing one's experience, strengths, and hopes, about finishing well, not just talking about how to do well. We inspire others without fanfare or monetary compensation. Love for fellow humans and thankfulness for one's journey can generate a passion to inspire others. Inspiration demonstrates reality in a world seemingly filled with unknowns. It screams to the world—"look at me, have hope."

> Tragedy is a tool for the living to gain wisdom.
>
> —R. Kennedy

Inspiration resembles a circle. What we give away comes back. What we receive only strengthens our own inspiration and desire to extend that to others. The scripture tells us that we are blessed when we give or share (Acts 20:35). Inspiration is like that. In this way, inspiration benefits both the giver and the receiver. Individuals, who are the source of inspiration, by sharing their story, are reminded of the journey, where they were and

> Steps to the gift of inspiration:
> 1. Awareness of what you have gone through can instill hope in others
> 2. Thankfulness for your own spiritual journey
> 3. Willingness to share your experiences, strengths, and hope
> 4. Acceptance of what you have gone through
> 5. Love for others

where they have gone. They are again blessed by appreciation as they recall the events in their lives. When individuals realize they are a source of inspiration to others who are hurting, it is a type of benefit finding in the reality of trauma and tragedy.

Inspiration is encouragement. The diagnosis of cancer or the rigors of treatment and evaluation often produce a need for encouragement. Encouragement involves something that will touch the heart. The medical model falls short of tugging those heartstrings that provide encouragement to the suffering. Sometimes it is just a word that keeps us going. Other times an event or something anticipated gives us something to look forward to. More often a visual awareness helps. The sufferer can perceive that if another cancer patient is doing well, that they have a chance of doing well. Sometimes one knows they need encouragement and sometimes not. Encouragement provides a source for the courage needed to "keep on keeping on." Usually, the giver may not bestow intentional encouragement. This reflects the spiritual realm of interconnectedness of all God's children. When one needs something, another will be there to provide it. We must be sensitive to the spiritual workings going on all about us.

> Be sensitive to your spiritual environment. Tragedy often brings spiritual matters to the forefront.

Inspiration is leading by example. Only a person can demonstrate the ability to overcome. The strength of many support programs is that individuals suffering from the same problems share their strengths, joys, and hopes and by doing so extend the infrastructure of support to the newly diagnosed. When one feels life has stopped, or it is the end of the road, or there is no tomorrow, or life will never be good again—inspiration is indeed a breath of fresh air to the suffocating soul. A cancer survivor shouts the message to the world—"Look at me. I was like you a few years ago, and look at me now. Do you see cancer? No, you see life and enjoyment and happiness."

Inspiration is hopefulness. A newly diagnosed cancer patient experiences hope when a survivor shares his/her story. Hope closely aligns itself with faith. Faith is defined as the substance of things hoped for (Hebrews 11:1). For a newly diagnosed patient or one suffering from treatment side effects, just getting through another day may be all that is hoped for. We might wonder how to have the faith to get through another day. A cancer survivor then provides his or her story, and the suffering patient can identify.

Inspiration is a source of courage. A newly diagnosed patient, when cared for by a cancer survivor, hears his or her story, visualizes getting better, and develops hope. The hope provides a handle to faith. Such an encounter facilitates courage. The same fears and anxieties have been experienced. When a military commander leads the charge, he is an inspiration to those following. If a cancer patient shares his or her struggles and is a living example of overcoming, or at least dealing, with those struggles, it instills courage to the newly diagnosed.

As previously noted, inspiration involves faith. Faith that what happened to one can happen to another provides a start. The cancer survivor has faith he or she will help another. Inspiration may be viewed as a gift of the spirit in that healing occurs (1 Corinthians 12:8–11, Galatians 5:16, 22–25). Former cancer patients often have a gift of being able to listen to another in a compassionate and empathic way. The needy patient senses this. Individuals with cancer are connected through a common weakness, that is, cancer, and they will move toward a common strength of successful suffering.

The primary purpose of any spiritual gift is to edify God's children. Since church is not restricted to a building, opportunity is extended to all God's children to make use of edification and encouragement. Such spiritual processes can occur equally in a physician's office or store aisle.

Is not encouragement a type of healing? As the spirit is wounded by the stress of having cancer, so it can be healed by encouraging words from another whose spirit was similarly wounded. An evangelism of concern exists for those suffering like you have suffered. Worship includes encouraging those who believe. King David prayed that he knew he would be walking through the shadow of death (Psalm 23:4). We all do. It is not a question of if we will but when we do. David had faith and received encouragement. We have faith and receive encouragement. David encouraged others. We encourage others.

Inspiration. What an awe-inspiring, complex word! Inspiration does not intentionally draw attention to the one inspiring another. But it is intentional in the sense of helping another. We never know whom we will come in contact with today that is in need of what we have to say or vice verse. Inspiration gives the opportunity to pass it on or pay it forward.

Teena acts as an advocate for patients. She demonstrates leadership. Since she has battled cancer, her story contains integrity. Because she has survived or lived with her cancer, she inspires hope. She can demonstrate a changed life because of what happened to her. Since she views her life as being so much better than she ever imagined before cancer, she models transformation.

> A cancer patient's story contains integrity. The story can be believed.

Teena received a great gift. She shares this gift, which has powerful consequences with others. Teena inspires her physicians and co-workers. Teena's successful journey inspires one to try even when the odds are against them. Russell Conwell wished to never allow an opportunity to help another pass, and he wrote a book, *Acres of Diamonds*, which taught the opportunities that existed in one's backyard.[59]

Teena's "acres of diamonds" is her workplace.

Lean On Me

As the road ahead seems rugged
and the path is getting steep,
I feel that I can't make it
so my heart begins to weep.

Then I turn to see who's coming
to join me on my way.
I see it is my Jesus
and He slowly turns to say,

"Lean on me …
when you have no strength to stand.
When you feel you're going under,
hold tighter to my hand.
Lean on me …
when your heart begins to bleed.
When you know I'm all you have,
then you'll find I'm all you need."

Then when I felt that no one cared
if I lived or died,
and no one bothered asking why
I'd go alone to cry.

When the burden got so heavy
I could barely face the day,
I felt His arms around me
as I gently heard Him say,

"Lean on me …
when you have no strength to stand.
When you feel you're going under,
hold tighter to my hand.
Lean on me …
when your heart begins to bleed.
When you come to know I'm all you have,
then you'll find I'm all you need."

—Author unknown

Facing the Valley

Lynda knew her body better than anyone else. She knew something was wrong and wouldn't give up searching for the answer. When finally diagnosed with cancer, she set about doing "what she had to do." Surrounded by an astounding support group, she is battling her illness on a personal level with God. She and her husband have three children, two daughters and a son. She is active in church work and sings in choirs and directs the children's choir. She plays flute and piano. She was involved in a community band until her chemotherapy conflicted.

Colorectal Cancer

Lynda had been in good health most of her life. She was found to have blood in her stools on her routine gynecological exam. This had resolved ten days later. Subsequently, she experienced problems with defecation and urinary tract infection. She was having quite a bit of pain and was admitted to the hospital a few months later. Attempts were made to perform a colonoscopy, and this could not be done due to the presence of a mass. She underwent surgery and had part of her colon resected, and the pathology revealed adenocarcinoma with lymph node involvement. She was treated with standard chemotherapy for six months and remained disease-free for almost two years.

Lynda's CEA (carcinoembryonic antigen, a tumor marker) value increased, and CT scan revealed disease in the liver. She was referred to a medical center for evaluation for resection of the liver disease, but she was found to have multiple pulmonary nodules and was deemed unresectable. She continued on different chemotherapy regimens and would initially respond only to have progressive disease after a few treatments. She was not eligible for a clinical trial.

Lynda lost her battle with colon cancer a little more than four years after her diagnosis. She remained a positive individual throughout her battle and remained active as long as possible in church and civic activities, as well as with her family. Her strong faith intensified during her trials, and her wish was that everyone would come to know God. She possessed the peace that surpasses all understanding.

LYNDA'S STORY

You have to get up every morning believing that God is in control and knowing that is the way it is. You have to do your part and be ready to fight.

Somebody at my church asked me, "How do you do this?"

I said, "You do what you have to do." Now, I could clean off a spot in the floor and have a pity party, but it wouldn't do any good.

> When you are alone, you are not. He is there. God is with you through others and through his creation and most importantly through his Spirit.

I was diagnosed about four years ago with colon cancer. I was feeling bad and had been to my OB/GYN physician in June for a regular checkup. He found some blood in the stool and said, "Now, this does not mean you have colon cancer. We are going to repeat the test in ten days." And in ten days, it was negative. I asked him if I should have a colonoscopy, and he said, "No." Plus, I really had started feeling better. Then, in September, I developed a bladder infection. I went back to my doctor for three consecutive weeks because I just could not get well.

That was when I knew something was going on. A bladder infection should not be that difficult to treat. Eventually the bladder infection got better, but then I couldn't sit comfortably anywhere. The pain would shift from the vaginal area to the rectal area. There was no position that was not painful.

Since I knew something had to be done, I went to see a surgeon who told me, "I see your problem. It's a fissure. Use this medication, and I will see you in two weeks." That was on Wednesday. That night, I was working with my children's choir at church. I started getting terribly sick. I went home, and I was throwing up and having diarrhea at the same time. I called my husband and said, "You have to come get me. Something is wrong!"

He took me to the emergency room, and I was admitted with gastroenteritis. The next day, they released me, but I still did not feel right. So in the meantime, there was a two-week span before I was to see the surgeon again. And still, I wasn't feeling right. At my two-week visit, I told him what I was feeling, and that's when he said, "Let's do a colonoscopy." And they found the tumor.

We know our bodies better than anybody else. If your doctor doesn't do what you need, find another doctor. Be persistent.

I don't remember feeling anything when they told me I had colon cancer. I didn't feel anger. I didn't feel fear. I just didn't feel anything. It was like, okay, here I am now. What are we going to do about this? I was numb as far as emotions go. This had been going on long enough, and I was ready to get going with whatever had to be done. I was never on an emotional roller coaster. I just accepted it.

I will tell you that I can't imagine going through this without knowing God on a personal level. My family has been supportive of me. Sometimes they even smother me with kindness and affection. I have to tell them to get back a little. I have to keep on living. I am here and I am okay. God has revealed that it is more than sunshine when I look out; it is God's creation. It is to marvel at. It is to be in awe of. It is to be absorbed.

For example, several weeks back, I felt really bad because this treatment I am getting is so terrible. It was the deepest, darkest night, and I was in the bed. My husband was at work, and I couldn't sleep and started thinking, "I just can't do this." Then God revealed an image to me. It was like I could reach out and touch this young man. It was the image of a wonderful young man with just the finest character from Tuscumbia, Alabama, who was killed in a tragic car accident last year. He spoke to me, "It's okay. You can do it." That was as real to me as this desk I am writing on.

I feel blessed all the time. I look outside and see the sunshine that is God's creation. The grass is a different shade of green now. The raindrops are a little bit wetter. I just appreciate things more. Even when I don't feel good, I am blessed because I could feel worse.

I have such a large support group. I can't count them all: my daughter's church, my son's church, my other daughter's church, my own church, my Sunday school class, and people that I don't even know.

One of the most important things to happen to me since this diagnosis is finding out how many friends I have. I didn't realize I had that many. I knew they would be nice to me and speak to me, but there is a difference now.

To say I have grown as a person is an understatement. I feel like my purpose is to tell everybody that I come into contact with, "You need to know the Lord." We are all going to face a valley. You can't appreciate the mountaintop until you have been down in that valley. You have to see how strong you really are. You are going to face it. The next person is going to face it, and you have got to be ready for it. You have to dig deep, very deep. Knowing God on a personal basis gives you the inner strength that is necessary for what lies ahead.

Cancer is a terrible thing, but it can be worse. I come from a family of seven, and I have two sisters who lost children to cystic fibrosis. One lost two and the other lost one. It, too, is a very ugly disease. I see a little boy who has cancer and think that is totally unfair for that child to have to go through this, but that's not my decision. And God has made him a ray of sunshine when I see him.

The spirit of the human being will change you if you allow it. We are going to see these people again, in heaven. That's exciting to me.

I have a very dear friend in Sunday school class who said, "It's going to be okay, no matter what happens." And it is. God provides the courage to deal with the problems at hand. I have done what God wanted me to do.

Just put your faith and trust where it should have always been. When we are Christians and something bad happens to us, we want to scream and yell and blame God and blame circumstances around us. You can't do that for very long. God will provide the strength that is necessary.

I live by Isaiah 41:10 (NKJV): "Fear not, for I am with thee. Be not dismayed for I am your God. I will strengthen you. Yes, I will help you and I will uphold you by my righteous hand." What more can I want?

THE GIFT OF ACCEPTANCE

Lynda's statement: "You have to get up every morning believing that God is in control and knowing that is the way it is. You have to do your part and be ready to fight," sounds like her mission statement. The components of her gift (acceptance) include (1) realizing who is in control (God), (2) accepting that she is not in control of much of her life, and (3) reaching the conclusion that, since this has happened to her, what does she do.

Wow! How can acceptance be a gift? Most individuals don't want to accept many life situations or circumstances. Why not? Problems are part of living. Some problems can be changed, but the majority cannot. Lynda, like quite a few struggling individuals, eventually comes to ask, "Why use energy to wage war against what I cannot change?" Acceptance frees us from having to wage war against "what is," and plan battles against "what ifs." We cannot change the fact of having been diagnosed with cancer or suffering from some other disease or set of circumstances. However, we can change our response to it. Acceptance is a choice made by individuals that seem to cope better.[60]

Acceptance is closely related to control. We live in a control-oriented world with voices from all viewpoints crying, "Take control of your life!" Control is not about forcing events and issues to come out the way we envision. Control is more about realizing we are not in control of most situations. If you think you are in control, make a list. The only thing we are in control of is how we respond.

> The only thing we are in control of is how we respond to life's events, and our initial response may be out of our control.

Acceptance, paradoxically, actually gives us more control, or at least lets us direct energies to the next right decision. Acceptance, in some programs, is viewed as the only way to stay healthy: "And acceptance is the answer to all my problems today. When I am disturbed, it is because I find some person, place, thing or situation—some fact of my life—unacceptable to me, and I can find no serenity until I accept that person, place, thing or situation as being exactly the way it is supposed to be at this moment. Nothing, absolutely nothing happens in God's world by mistake."[61] Acceptance is often facilitated by repeated attempts at failure to control.

Acceptance involves a level of discernment. In the Serenity Prayer,[62] "wisdom to know the difference" refers to what can be changed and what cannot be changed. A plan of action follows. If we know what we have control over, we can develop a plan of action or, in much broader terms, a plan of life. At some point or the other, each of us faces the following question: What can be changed and what cannot be changed? Many of life's difficulties are caused by the inability to distinguish between these two. Traumatic events or life-threatening illness can be a catalyst to discernment.

> Steps to the gift of acceptance:
> 1. Realize who is in control of what
> 2. Acceptance of what you are not in control of
> 3. Decide to use your energy purposefully
> 4. Become aware of how you have responded to difficult events in the past
> 5. Focus thoughts on the good of any event

Most people will eventually realize the value of acceptance. However, the big question of "How does this work?" remains. Although the benefit of acceptance may not be understood, it can be appreciated.

Others may remark, "This acceptance stuff isn't working for me. What's the secret?"

For some, acceptance seems natural, probably because they have done it often in facing other difficult circumstances. For those of us who have not had the opportunity to practice acceptance, "How does it work?" can be a daunting question. We struggle to obtain the unobtainable, achieve the unachievable, to be the person we are not able to be, and so on. Much of life is a struggle against acceptance. The serenity prayer is a wonderful aide to internalizing this gift. When facing a new trauma or difficult life event, I have found it helpful to repeat it several times a day. While familiar with the first verse, fewer know the other words of wisdom, like, "accepting hardships as a pathway to peace."

Any problem or life-changing event, such as cancer, is really a set of circumstances that threatens our well-being at that moment. We often bring to that event the mind-set that the presence of positive circumstances represents happiness, and the absence of positive or the presence of negative circumstances represents sadness. Is this valid? Not really. Happiness and sadness result largely from our responses to circumstances.

Acceptance is closely related to serenity or contentment. How successful are we at getting other people and events where we want them? We are not. Thus, our frustrations begin, and use much of our energy and life. The frustrations give rise to resentment, anger, fear, lack of forgiveness, bitterness, and gossip. Our "home remedies" for our inability to change people and things include blaming others and justifying ourselves, self-pity (really self-centered behavior), increased visits to health care professionals, submitting to addictive behavior, involving a neutral person (such as pastor), or attacking God. The spiritual remedy for turning discontentment into contentment is acceptance of circumstances that cannot be changed.

Acceptance can become a lifestyle that extends beyond circumstances or a trial such as cancer. Acceptance leads to contentment. If we are content and peaceful only when things are going our way, then we will be discontent most of the time. Contentment is a learned response (Philippians 4:11–13). A learned response involves growing accustomed to a circumstance or event by experiencing it, being aware of our response to it, and knowing if we should accept or change it. Learned responses come from correct thinking. What we think about certainly controls our lives, so we need to develop the habit of correct thinking. Six qualities assist us in correct thinking.[63] "Is it true?"

Six qualities help us in correct thinking:
1. Tell the truth
2. Give reverence to what is worthy
3. Do what is right
4. Practice moderation
5. Promote peacefulness
6. Leave a legacy of integrity

"Is it noble?" "Is it right?" "Is it pure?" "Is it lovely?" "Is it admirable?" If right thinking (Philippians 4:8–9) leads to right behaviors, then we must practice, through constant repetition, to develop the skill.

Acceptance means we lack control over some or many events and circumstances. You may ask, "Then what do we have control over?" At first, it appears we have control over three things: our thoughts, our actions, and our words. However, thoughts can just appear randomly, so we do not control our thoughts, but we have control over our obsession of our thoughts. Likewise, we sometimes say things we wish we had not said, and we do things we wish we had not done. Thus, we only have control over the things we choose to dwell on.

Cancer has been a source of growth for Lynda. She can honestly say, "I have grown as a person is an understatement. I feel like my purpose is to tell everybody that I come into contact with, 'You need to know the Lord.'" Like some other patients, Lynda has experienced a renewed urgency to share her relationship with God. We are made in the image of God, and, perhaps, we have control over making the decision to know God and to allow him to control our lives. Some will ask, "Why do I have to accept the circumstances if prayer changes things?" Letting God control our lives does not lead to a life of passivity. Our lives become dynamic because we remove the clutter of human nature and free our spiritual inheritance to manifest itself. We need to be who God wants us to be, and not who we think God wants us to be.

Paul tells the Christians at Philippi that he has learned to be content in all things. Yet the same Paul also talked about being a very wretched man (Romans 7:24). At a time when his life was out of control, Paul achingly described his misery. What changed Paul? Whatever (or whoever) changed Paul can change us. Just as God redirected Paul, he can redirect us. God works to redirect our lives to where he wants us to go. However, we don't always respond to ensure we are going in that direction.

I do not fully understand this since God does not cause cancer in one and heart disease in another. However, I do know that if a person is seeking God, that person's life will be changed for the better as a result of having cancer. God wants us to be content. He wants us to experience the "peace that surpasses all understanding" (Philippians 4:7).

> Trust God moment by moment even when we don't understand his ways. Life is a mystery to be experienced rather than to be understood.

As we travel our path to contentment, we must become accepting of those things we cannot change, we must accept God's calling to change those things he has called us to change, and we must accept our situation in life so that, like Lynda, if we could change it, we would choose not to do so. It is helpful if we trust God moment by moment without necessarily understanding his ways, and be thankful for what God does and allows in our lives.

DAILY ACCEPTANCE PRAYER

I accept myself completely.
I accept my strengths and my weaknesses,
my gifts and my shortcomings,
my good points and my faults.

I accept myself completely as a human being.
I accept that I am here to learn and grow, and
I accept that I am learning and growing.
I accept the personality I've developed, and
I accept my power to heal and change.

I accept myself without condition or reservation.
I accept that the core of my being is goodness and
that my essence is love, and
I accept that I sometimes forget that.

I accept myself completely, and in this acceptance
I find an ever-deepening inner strength.
From this place of strength, I accept my life fully and
I open to the lessons it offers me today.

I accept that within my mind are both fear and love, and
I accept my power to choose which I will experience as real.
I recognize that I experience only the results of my own choices.

I accept the times that I choose fear
as part of my learning and healing process, and
I accept that I have the potential and power
in any moment to choose love instead.

I accept mistakes as a part of growth,
so I am always willing to forgive myself and
give myself another chance.

I accept that my life is the expression of my thought, and
I commit myself to aligning my thoughts
more and more each day with the Thought of Love.
I accept that I am an expression of this Love.
Love's hands and voice and heart on earth.

I accept my own life as a blessing and a gift.
My heart is open to receive, and I am deeply grateful.
May I always share the gifts that I receive
fully, freely, and with joy.

—Author unknown[64]

Feeling Lucky

Today, thirty-eight-year-old Mary Alice feels great. But just three years ago, she faced a diagnosis of lung cancer and brain metastasis. Short of a miracle, she believes she is still here because God did not give her more than she could handle. Even at her lowest point, she knew she would be here for her son and her mother because they needed her.

Squamous Cell Lung Cancer

Non-small cell lung cancer generally carries a poor prognosis, especially when metastatic. The most common cause of lung cancer is smoking cigarettes. Mary Alice smoked and knew she had contributed to the cancer she was now battling. She was thirty-six years old. Almost four years ago, she was diagnosed with squamous cell carcinoma of the lung. She had experienced a rapid swelling of her neck and upper chest area. This is called superior vena cava syndrome when associated with malignancy. She had extensive mediastinal adenopathy and a mass in the right upper lobe of her lung.

Superior vena cava syndrome is an oncologic emergency, and she was started on radiation therapy and chemotherapy immediately. After she completed the chemotherapy treatment, she had a seizure and was found to have metastatic disease in the brain. She was started on steroids due the edema present and underwent Gamma Knife (a type of radiation treatment in which intense doses of radiation are given to the targeted area of cancer).

She was initially treated with weekly chemotherapy while receiving radiation therapy. The superior vena cava syndrome improved, and after completion of radiation treatment, her chemotherapy drugs and frequency of administration was changed. She received five cycles of chemotherapy. Her treatments were complicated by chemotherapy-related anemia requiring transfusions as well as a nonmalignant pericardial effusion requiring surgery and drainage.

She has been disease-free about four years. Mary Alice remains optimistic and continues to advocate a nonsmoking lifestyle. Her mother and son were a reason for her desire to live, and the family continues to rely on each other.

Mary's Story

I am a thirty-eight-year-old single parent with an eighteen-year-old son. I was thirty-five years old when my journey with cancer started. I was laid off at the screen-printing place where I had worked for thirteen years. The company moved overseas and left me without a job. Thankfully, though, I was able to keep my insurance active.

I was having neck pain. It woke me up, and the pain was very intense. I just wanted to die. That night, my son had a basketball game. I have never missed any of his games and didn't want to miss that one, either. So I called my mother and asked her if she had anything for pain. She told me "no" because she knew something was wrong with me, since I never took medicine. She also told me, "You are going to the hospital." I went to the emergency room at the hospital, and they told me I had whiplash. The doctor said he could see swelling, so he made an appointment with a bone doctor. But I told Momma, "It's not my bones."

It was in awful throbbing pain. I could not stand it. The swelling started moving, and we could watch it move across my body. It went over into my right arm, and my arm got so big, I thought it would burst. My mother called a surgeon, and he thought it might be a blood clot and recommended a CT scan. After the test, they admitted me to the hospital.

Then, I met a lung doctor. He told us I did have blood clots, and some spots were showing up that could be cancer. He explained that the only way to know for sure is to do a biopsy. They did the biopsy, and when they came into my room to tell me it was lung cancer, everything in the whole room just went blank. The only thing I could see was my son's face. I wanted to live for him.

I thought of my grandmother who died from lung cancer. She smoked. I smoked, too. At that point, all I could think was, "Oh, my God, I am going to die." The doctor told me he could put the smoking patches on me or write a prescription to help me stop smoking. He also told me if I smoked, it was going to kill me. So I went cold turkey and quit.

> The diagnosis of cancer produces an intense crisis and can be a strong motivation to change behavior, either to stop something not healthy or to begin something that is healthy.

It was not really me that I was worried about—it was my son. His dad owed us so much money on back child support. I thought, "This is going to be worse on my son than me." We have always been very close.

It hit my mother hard, too. We lost my brother in a car wreck when he was seventeen, and mom didn't want to lose me too. She asked the doctors if I could have her lung, but they said it wouldn't work. It didn't look good for me in the beginning. My mother and my surviving brother and I were always very close as a family.

I went through a lot of scans and tests. The blood clots were from the lung cancer. I was going to be treated with radiation and chemotherapy. The term used by the doctors was superior vena cava syndrome.

When I started my radiation treatments, one of the first people I met was an old friend of my older brother's from school. I will never forget what he said. He told me not to worry about my hair or anything else because he had seen a lot of people go through this

> Strong emotions are associated with the diagnosis of cancer, such as fear, hopelessness, helplessness, and anxiety. In addition to the experience of the vulnerability to the disease, patients experience unfamiliar technology, difficulty navigating the healthcare delivery system, and a continuous exposure to "unknowns."

and it is 98 percent up to you. I thought, "Well, if that is so, then this is going to be easy." So that is how I felt—like I was not sick.

I completed the chemotherapy and radiation therapy. Not long afterward, I had to go the hospital. I was very short of breath and had chest pain, and was very weak. I felt dizzy. I had fluid around my heart, and I had to have surgery and the fluid drained. I was relieved when cancer cells were not found.

Not long afterward, I started to feel real funny, and I told my dad my legs felt numb. My mom called. She had just left and not been gone long. She asked how I was doing, and I told her the same thing and that

I didn't know how to explain it. She told me that is what her mother said before she passed away, and she turned around and came right back.

All that day I had felt "out of body." It seemed like I was in the bed and the door was on the right side, but it seemed like everybody was going out the left side of me. It is just hard to explain. I couldn't feel my arm. It was dead weight. And it scared me to death. I called my mom and went to the emergency room. I laugh about it now because I would put my arm on the back of the car seat and it would give away, and I would hit the driver. After I got to the hospital, I had a seizure. The nurses thought I had a stroke because they had never seen a seizure that bad. The scans showed that the cancer had gone to my brain and caused the seizure.

I just couldn't feel my arm. They told me most likely I would lose the function of my arm. But after the Gamma Knife therapy, when they woke me, I could raise my arm after all. I was so happy. That was over two years ago and things have been great since.

I had been through chemo and radiation, sick and down, but I believe when I did not have the use of my arm, that bothered me more than anything. There were so many things I could not do. I couldn't bathe, get dressed, or shave my legs. It made me look at other people that are handicapped and wonder how they do it. I saw myself, but then I saw others even worse. I felt blessed.

I was never bitter. I just accepted it. I didn't feel sorry for myself. Cancer runs in my family. It is part of life for my family. Even my great-grandfather had bone cancer. I smoked. I did not eat right. I felt like I did not have anyone to blame but myself. I decided to deal with it myself. I have read stories about people with cancer feeling sorry for themselves. I never did that. I accepted what had happened. I accepted the bad choices I had made about smoking. You know, I really felt like I did not have anyone to blame but myself. I see so many people going through cancer treatments who still smoke, and I try to talk to them, whether they agree or not. They do listen to me, though.

> Steps for successful suffering:
> 1. Take ownership of your role
> 2. Identify the spiritual lessons that may be involved
> 3. Do the next right thing with God's help

My cancer has shown me a lot of things. My son was the perfect kid, and then he did some things he should not have, but I think he is a better person now. Some kids wait until they get out of high school to do wrong things. Now, my son is enrolled to go to college this summer. Last year, he worked two jobs at seventeen years old, and there are not too many seventeen-year-olds who do that. He is writing music and playing in a band.

I think he has learned a lot. I have been a single mother for so long, and I would always worry about bills and money. One time, we pulled up at the grocery store, and a homeless man was sitting in the corner by the soft drink machine, and my son said, "Well, Momma, you know that it could be a lot worse." I looked over and he was showing me that man, and it made me feel so bad. I thought, you know, we have a home. We have supper. My son is a great person.

Yes, in the beginning, it was overwhelming. I prayed to God and asked him to just let me see my son graduate, and then I would ask him for more things. I told Momma we always seem to ask God for more and more. We believed that God would provide the strength to get through what had to be done. I give God the praise for allowing me to continue to live.

> Bargaining can be beneficial. It gives us goals to work toward, and teaches dependence on God.

Now, most people wouldn't even know I am sick. I honestly don't feel like anything is wrong with me. I have survived it. My friends say, "My goodness, you are still smiling." I am so thankful I can be independent. I did not like having other people wait and care for me. When it looked like my arm might be paralyzed, I hated that. But when the Gamma Knife treatment was over, and I could raise my arm, I said, "Thank you, God."

I just feel so fortunate. That is how I look at it. Now I live each day to its fullest. I do the best I can do. I don't have to worry about today or the day I leave here. I just feel so lucky. You know, God will take care of that day. Only God knows when that day comes. I am comfortable and don't worry about it. I want to live at peace with all. If a problem arises, we need to straighten it out. What if something happened to me and I was in the middle of an argument?

I am blessed. I am fortunate. I have a positive mental attitude.

The Gift of Beneficial Attitude

"I was never bitter. I just accepted it. I didn't feel sorry for myself. Cancer runs in my family. It is part of life for my family. Even my great-grandfather had bone cancer. I smoked. I did not eat right. I felt like I did not have anyone to blame but myself." Mary's statement covers a variety of gifts that have come about by her diagnosis and by her awareness of cancer as fairly common in her family. Mary demonstrates an attitude of acceptance, serenity, and ownership of her situation.

Attitude is just as important in everyday living as it is when we face a traumatic event or crisis. Defining attitude, either positive or negative, is harder than observing who has which one. But let's try to examine what an attitude is, whether attitudes are beneficial or harmful, and whether attitudes can be changed. Undoubtedly, if a certain attitude is beneficial, the question becomes how to intervene in order that more people experience that attitude. But if a particular attitude is harmful, how do we prevent that attitude?

Composed of what one thinks, how one feels, and what one does, attitude simply describes how an individual responds to a situation. For example, an evaluation of Mary's attitude about cancer is composed of three questions: (1) What does Mary think about having cancer? (2) What does Mary feel about having cancer? (3) What is Mary going to do about having cancer?

Although all people, whether characterized as having a positive or negative attitude, may eventually develop Mary's coping strategy, let's examine Mary's attitude. Mary's attitude includes ownership of her contribution to the fact she developed lung cancer. She did not blame anyone but herself. This is such a contrast to those who come into the office with the diagnosis of lung cancer, and have a pack of cigarettes in their pocket or the smell of cigarette smoke on their person, and want to blame and file a lawsuit against their employer. Taking ownership of one's own behavior is difficult and reflects an honest self-examination.

Mary has adjusted to the cancer experience. She realizes she may not live, but she remains hopeful and optimistic. She set a goal of seeing her son graduate from high school. She now is setting other goals. Mary has identified her support system, a valuable component of a good attitude.

Her support system of her family and God helped and continue to help her maintain a positive attitude.

Mary also experiences and discusses what many call negative emotions or attitudes. She holds her emotions in balance, and they do not cripple or hinder her enjoying life. A balance of emotional states may be more important than a positive attitude. Let me explain. Balance deals with experiencing both positive and negative emotions. Once a negative attitude is sensed, it needs to be dealt with. It does not need to be suppressed. Thus, a balanced state is one in which the negative attitude is not suppressed, but felt, experienced, and hopefully resolved, while positive attitudes are enhanced.

Most believe that patients suffering from life-threatening diseases need positive attitudes. Historically, both laypeople and professionals have implied that a good attitude helps fight cancer. However, we do not fully understand all the details. Recent studies demonstrated that a positive attitude had no effect on how long one lived. An Australian study reported that an optimistic attitude didn't prolong the survival of non-small cell lung cancer patients.[65] Similarly, a larger study of more than one thousand individuals being treated for head and neck cancer showed the emotional state of the patients had no influence on survival.[66]

These studies, however, do not address what effect attitude might have on the development of disease up to the time of diagnosis, nor on the quality of life that is experienced by those individuals. That is, could a positive outlook, say, in young adulthood, protect against death or, at least, could it prolong survival?

Regardless, the lack of benefit from a positive attitude on survival is an important finding and could provide hope to those who do not feel positive. With the popular notion that a positive outlook and attitude goes a long way in beating cancer, the patient has felt inadequate and deflated if he or she is not in the "positive attitude category." Families have blamed loved ones for not having the "right attitude" to ensure cancer survival. Involvement in psychotherapy support groups has also been shown not to influence survival.[67] At the same time, involvement does impart an improved quality of life.[68]

> Not all patients can demonstrate a positive attitude. It is best to accept that rather than induce more stress by trying to have something you do not have.

Caution is in order. Such pinpointed studies may be misleading. Attitudes develop around an event. The event is cancer. One wants to beat it. One may have developed a positive attitude as a result of cancer. Longitudinal studies, in which the attitude of an individual has been determined at various points along life, are more valid. And in this respect, numerous studies demonstrate a survival advantage and years added when a positive attitude is maintained over a long period of time.

Other studies have demonstrated an increased life span associated with a life of living with a positive attitude. A study of Catholic nuns strongly associated the positive emotional content of autobiographies written at twenty-two years of age with survival.[69] Additional studies associated positive and negative attitudes with health and life span.[70] Positive mental attitude appears to be a key in surviving.[71]

> A positive attitude throughout life results in an increased life span, improved quality of life, and many other health benefits.

To be sure, longevity relates to more than a positive attitude. Factors such as gender, genetics, socioeconomic status, church attendance, support systems, lifestyle choices, temperament, personality, and traumatic events are all involved in how long one lives.[72,73] We are beginning to appreciate the mechanisms for such positive benefits. For example, emotions influence the autonomic nervous system and may influence health. Interestingly, suppression of emotions, which might be viewed by others as a positive attitude, negatively affects health. We can also associate an optimistic attitude with overall feelings of well-being and perhaps a longer life.[74] A study of 839 patients from the Mayo Clinic associated optimism with a lower risk of death over a period of three decades.[75] The aging process in general may be dependent on one's attitude toward aging; a positive attitude added over seven years to the life span.[76]

Perhaps the more important question relates a positive attitude and quality of life. Most still believe a positive, upbeat attitude is important in coping with cancer. While it is important to live as long as you can, it may be more important to live as well as you can while living as long as you can. Most of us favor quality of life over length of life. What does quality of life involve? It includes the physical, functional, social, emotional, and spiritual. The qualities occur within the context of the individual's personality, the support network, the goals desired, and the means by which to accomplish these goals, and they differ from individual to individual.

This brings us to our third question: "Can attitudes be changed?" Healthcare professionals ask themselves, "How can we help patients move from a negative to a positive attitude?" Changing our attitude involves changing how we think about an event, how we feel about it, or what we are doing about it. The big question is which one do you attempt to change first, or do you try to change all three? Perhaps the best approach to attitude change is to change what is easiest first. Pick the lowest hanging fruit. Gain knowledge about the event or action related to the event and then use it. For example, Mary immediately stopped smoking. She took the knowledge and changed a behavior. She took ownership of what role she had played in combination with genetic contribution. She changed knowledge. And she did something different.

But changing how we think and what we do may be a great deal easier than changing how we feel. What happens when we hear the word "cancer"? It is sense of impending doom. Emotions flood the person. We may feel angry, sad, fearful, stressed, anxious, frustrated, scared, or all the above. Having strong emotions can even make us feel terrible, and many view the expression of these feelings as weakness. Many patients stuff their feelings and put up a front. So many times, I have heard the statement: "I've got to be strong for my family." At this point, some will try to numb these feelings by increasing use of alcohol or drugs or other addictive behavior. Medicines are prescribed to block these "bad" feelings, and patients are not given the opportunity to feel, and they are not provided with skills in dealing with possible emotional responses to cancer. Sometimes, the angry, hurtful emotions are expressed, not at the cancer, but at our loved ones, or at God.

> Changing how we feel is more difficult than changing how we think or how we behave.

When emotions or feelings are strong, we more easily notice, or others more readily notice, our attitudes. For example, upon hearing the word "cancer," fear is a frequently experienced emotion. If we try to not have fear, fear often intensifies. The thought associated with the feeling must be examined. We make changing our attitudes harder by focusing on the most difficult component, the feelings. You may ask, "How can one change a feeling?" Exactly. Changing feelings is far from easy. Even defining a feeling is hard. So the approach to changing feelings requires us to grasp the thoughts and actions associated with the attitude, not to focus on the feeling involved. This method works because thoughts, actions, and feelings are intertwined. They are really inseparable. So changing the easiest will eventually change the most difficult.

The questions become "How do we change what we think?" and "How do we change what we do?" Let me share a personal experience. I used to smoke. I tried many times to stop smoking. But I enjoyed smoking. I tried to tell myself not to enjoy smoking. I knew the risks of smoking. I had known them for years. I even cared for patients who had cancer related to their smoking. This actually involved a change in thinking because as the son of a tobacco farmer, smoking was a way of life. Prior to becoming a physician, I knew the reports on the effects of smoking and made excuses and the usual governmental blames. It took many years for my thinking to change, and even more years for my actions to change. I didn't smoke at work or in the house, but eventually,

Steps to having a beneficial attitude:
1. Feel the negative feelings and deal with them
2. Experience, embellish, and enjoy your positive feelings
3. Be aware of how your body responds to different events
4. Anticipate positive outcomes
5. Take ownership of your contribution to the event
6. Minimize self-pity
7. Keep a list of attainable goals you are striving for

sneaking smoke breaks became too much. A change of action followed, especially when I discovered that the incredible urge to smoke was short-lived. I needed to do something, anything, other than smoke for a few minutes. What would I do? I decided to pray for other people—their welfare and life improvement. It worked.

Okay. You may be thinking, "I need to fill my life with positive attitudes. I need a plan." We all do, and here it is: (1) Feel your negative feelings. Express them, experience them, and move on. (2) Feel your positive feelings. Then express them, experience them, embellish them, and enjoy them. (3) Learn your body. How does your body respond differently to negative versus positive emotions? (4) Appreciate the fact that as you recover from the traumatic experience of cancer or other event, there is a good chance you will be more optimistic about life, your life will have more meaning and purpose, and you will have learned to count your blessings.

Some may think, "This hasn't happened for me." Perhaps it has not happened completely, but the fact that you are aware of it is a step on your spiritual journey. Some may need to see a trained counselor. Some may need medication. However, be careful of medications that serve only to numb one's feelings. Numbing your feeling may be counterproductive.

How does a positive attitude look in the real world of bad events? Let's look at Mary's story again. Mary quickly found meaning in her disease and purpose in living. The diagnosis of cancer made her stop smoking, and she starting talking to people about not smoking. She found meaning in the fact that she had a seizure because it brought attention to the cancer in her brain. Mary uses her faith to deal with negative emotions. Mary is also realistic. She is constantly reminded that she may die, and she even uses this to encourage her family. Mary counts her blessings daily. When we do this, a more positive attitude seems to follow. Perhaps Mary's life resembles the title to a David Woodward song. She maintains an "Attitude of Gratitude."

> Count your blessings frequently and a more positive attitude will follow. How frequently? When you are feeling down.

What You See Is What You Get [77]

Your life at any time can become difficult.
Your life at any time can become easy.
It all depends upon how you adjust yourself to life.
Positive thinking is simply reacting positively to a negative situation.
So try to see the good in every situation.
You cannot always control your circumstances.
But you can control your own thoughts.
Things seem to turn out best for those people
who can make the best out of the way things turn out.
It's not the situation,
It's your reaction to the situation.
The reality of your life may result from many outside factors,
none of which you can control.
Your attitude, however,
reflects the ways in which you elevate what is happening to you.
What has happened to you,
good or bad,
only your thinking makes it so.

—Author unknown

This Is the End of My Life

Cancer-free for seventeen years, Willie knows all about God's timing. Now, at age sixty-six, Willie lives in a state of peace and constant joy. With two sons and three grandchildren, she now works for God, and she believes wholeheartedly that her breast cancer made her a stronger person.

Advanced Breast Cancer

Willie was diagnosed with stage III breast cancer. She was scared at the mention of cancer. She lost all hope that she could ever be healthy again. She had undergone multiple breast biopsies, which always came back as benign. She visited her surgeon, who again felt several masses in her left breast. The mammogram showed nodular densities that were new. An aspiration was done, and atypical cells were seen. Willie underwent excisional biopsy, and she was shocked when she was told she had cancer. Willie's cancer was intraductal carcinoma. She saw an oncologist who presented what Willie referred to as the cold facts of breast cancer. She was even more terrified. She lost all hope. She was depressed.

Willie came to our office for a second opinion. Even though we recommended the same drugs as the first physician, Willie found hope because she heard words emphasizing survival over relapse, disease-free status over disease recurrence, and tips on how to manage side effects if they occurred.

It has been seventeen years since Willie started chemotherapy. The hope she received on her first visit gave her the necessary strength, courage, and desire to proceed. She received eight cycles of chemotherapy. She has been disease-free since completion of her treatment. She experienced some of the side effects, but they were short-lived.

Willie enjoys life more than ever. She attributes her battle with cancer as the beginning of new strength and faith. She shares that with whomever she sees. She remains active in church.

WILLIE'S STORY

I had finished moving to a new place. I thought the soreness in my chest was from the move: lifting, reaching, and stretching. But the pain was getting worse and was waking me up at night. I felt against my breast, and I said, "Hum, that feels funny." The pain ran up under my arm. I made an appointment with the surgeon I had seen because of fibrocystic disease. A mammogram was done and then a biopsy.

I was told I had breast cancer. I could not believe this was happening to me. I cried, "Why me?"

I went home, fell across the bed, and cried out. I thought, "Yes, this is the end of my life here. It's all over." I just couldn't believe that it was happening to me. I kept thinking, "Why me?"

I saw an oncologist. I had been told how serious the situation was and that I would be undergoing aggressive chemotherapy, and that it might not work. That was seventeen years ago, and I was diagnosed

> Spiritual people often feel hopeless. The hopelessness is not permanent. Sometimes we need to be like Abraham who hoped in spite of hopeless circumstances (Romans 4:18).

with stage III breast cancer. I felt so hopeless. It was a sleepless night. My mind was racing and couldn't stop.

Around four o'clock in the morning, I thought about a verse in the Bible, the one with the three lepers who say to each other, "Why sit here until we die?" They said, "Let's go to the city gates" (2 Kings 7:3). The verse was a source of inspiration for me. So I decided I was not going to crawl up in this bed and lie here and feel sorry for myself. If I died, I would do it trying to live, just like the lepers. And like them, I would depend on God to take care of me. I got up, looked around at what needed doing, and started washing clothes.

> Action is often associated with hope, and the decision for action can be hope-generating itself.

Then, on a recommendation, I went to see another cancer doctor. After talking to him, I realized there was hope. The same chemotherapy was recommended and the same side effects discussed, but they were discussed in a different manner. He emphasized the number of people who did not suffer side effects, and he emphasized living rather than dying. I went home and got alone with the Lord. I said, "God, I need a miracle. I know you are in the miracle-working business, and I am putting myself totally in your hands." When I said that, a peace came over me that I cannot explain to this day. And a joy. I had such a joy that even when I would go for treatments, knowing it was going to make me sick, it was just like nothing was going on with me.

I took chemotherapy from June through November. The nurses were wonderful, and my doctors. See, God had a hand in the whole thing. I have to give credit and praise to him. From the time I was recommended to the second oncology office, it was like God put me in line with all the people who knew him. I was encouraged to fight, to put up with the side effects. God worked through all of them. He just worked it all out, and through it all I had such a peace and joy that I can't explain even to this day. Although I knew bad things were happening, and the world was still going on, but I was over here in this secret place of the most high, sheltered up under the arms of the Almighty. It was like I am over here, and the world is still going on over there.

The nightmare of having cancer, when it became reality, strengthened my faith. I was not alone. I had heard about God all my life, but then I got to know him. He became more real to me. I knew that he loved me and he was going to care for me, and take care of me, and he did. God did some awesome things for me during that time.

> God becomes more real during a crisis because we become more dependent on him. We are redirected to a new place with him along our spiritual journey.

I kind of came into being. I got in touch with myself. I came to realize that I, through dependence on God, was stronger than I gave myself credit for and learned I could do and bear more. Fighting cancer made me stronger. Now, I could help other people. If someone comes to me and wants prayer, I go to the Lord and go to work for him or her.

I stand bold for them and encourage them. If they say, "Oh, I can't do that." I say, "Oh, yes, you can." I make them feel better to know there is somebody who is strong and has made it this long. This year, it is seventeen years cancer-free.

The biggest change in my life after my diagnosis has been my deeper understanding of God. I have a thirst for him. I knew him before as God; now, I know him as my Father. You know, God has timing for us. Every diagnosis you get is not the sentence of death. I learned that. I was more afraid of cancer before my diagnosis, because I had always thought there was no way to survive it. I didn't know people who had survived cancer. Now, I can encourage people to get their mammograms and to take care of themselves a little better.

But I surrounded myself with things of God. I would listen to tapes and read. I would listen to music, anything that would lift my spirit. I never accepted the negative. Even when I got a negative report, like my blood count would be low, I would come home and get my book and say, "No, this is what the word of God says about me."

I respected and loved my doctors, and I knew they had to give me their reports. But then, I would go to the "greatest Physician," and his word said different about me. I had a great support system. One lady in particular was of great support, and we were also prayer partners.

There is always hope with cancer.

The Gift of Hope

Willie knows the importance of hope. Willie said, "After talking to him, I realized there was hope." As her physician, I learned an important lesson on her first visit. After the treatment options were explained, along with possible risks and benefits, Willie looked at me and said, "At least you haven't taken away my hope." Her statement immediately became part of my "way of doing business." I realized the power of hope. What a difference in outlook simply because one doctor emphasized the chance of survival, rather than the chance of dying!

What is hope? Hope is such a powerful component of our being. Many see hope, along with faith and love, as a spiritual gift (1 Corinthians 13). When we analyze Willie's story, we can define hope more easily. First, we see an unsatisfactory present condition. This could be the diagnosis of cancer or any other traumatic, tragic, or turmoil-generating circumstance. Hope occurs in the midst of suffering, uncertainty, and stress.

> Hope occurs in the midst of suffering, uncertainty, and stress.

Second, we see uncertainty about the future. Willie thinks she is going to die because of the life-threatening issues associated with breast cancer. But Willie wants to live. She doesn't know if she will.

The third component of hope is a desired outcome. A hopeful individual believes the current situation will improve. Hope often transcends the physical. We know the possibility of a better condition.

Fourth, we view the desired outcome as reasonable; it can happen. Willie knows it is possible for people to live after undergoing treatment for breast cancer. She learns about people who have. Healthcare providers need to be a source of hope. The expectation does not ensure that the desired outcome will occur. Sources of information include the physician and patient stories. When true stories are presented to our patients, the patient develops a perspective of the possibilities, and the perspective impacts a patient's quality of life. Willie based her hope on stories that emphasized surviving. Each patient in a physician's office may be a source of hope for others. The physician needs to make use of the narratives and use them in sharing hope to others. Stories of hope are much better than statistics.

Rather than give up, Willie decided to go ahead with chemotherapy. She saw evidence that the outcome could be different than she initially believed, that is, that she would die. So Willie practices the fifth component of hope: she made a decision to act. But such a decision

> Steps to the gift of hope:
> 1. Realize the power of hope
> 2. Examine your possibilities
> 3. Maintain a realistic desired outcome
> 4. Take the next right step that is hope generating
> 5. Monitor for false hope
> 6. Share your story of hope

does not give power to hope unless one follows through with action. Therefore, Willie took action to achieve the desired outcome.

> Hope occurs in anticipation of an outcome's possibility, not with its assurance.

Whether the desired outcome happens or not, hope remains. Hope occurs in anticipation of the outcome's possibility, not with its assurance. Hope is independent of the outcome.

Meaning and purpose of life often operate alongside hope. With cancer, we increase our hopefulness to live longer, but we may also increase our significance in the world. And if we take action to enhance meaning and purpose of life, it often results in increased hopefulness. The action itself is "hope-generating." Hope manifests itself in actions designed to leave something good behind. For example, writing letters to loved ones, producing a DVD, spending time just talking, taking a special vacation, journaling, or sharing one's possessions indicate a need to provide a legacy to those we love.

Hope often expresses itself through relationships with self, others, and/or God. Hope involves the individual's family, as well. Families strive to demonstrate their hope as a source of encouragement and hope for the patient. They rarely give the appearance of losing hope because they see their "hope" as important to the patient they dearly love. Hope gives courage and the ability to "hang in there."

Hope is a choice. It is dynamic. It is constantly changing. An individual constantly reevaluates hope based on each day's new realities.

> Hope always occurs in the context of reality.

Hope always occurs in the context of reality. Hope also involves reconciling desired outcomes to life's actualities. For instance, when Willie first learned she needed a biopsy, the prevailing hope was that she would not have cancer. Once Willie learned she did have cancer, she hoped the cancer was not advanced. When the pathology report revealed advanced cancer, she hoped for a cure, and so on. Today, Willie remains cancer free, and she hopes her story will benefit others.

Hope replaces despair. Hope changes perspective. Hope provides the possibility of other outcomes, although the probabilities are unknown to us. Hope redirects our thinking toward new, sometimes unexpected, possibilities. When Pandora, according to Greek mythology, opened the box and allowed all evils to be released, she filled humankind with misery and despair. But alone at the bottom of the box remained hope. When she eventually released it, hope went wherever humanity felt pain and hopelessness. Hope gave mankind relief from all life's evils.

For many, hope is a meeting place of the secular and the sacred. Hope involves faith. Hope involves belief. Hope requires more than wishful thinking, and it involves evidence to the contrary of hopelessness. "Hope is the elevating feeling we experience when we see—in the mind's eye—a path to a better future. Hope acknowledges the significant obstacles and deep pitfalls along the path."[78] Hope is central to human flourishing and, at the same time, so difficult to understand or internalize. Alexander Pope wrote, "Hope springs eternal in the human breast."[79] O. S. Marden, founder of *Success Magazine*, expressed his thoughts on hope: "There is no medicine like hope, no incentive so great, and no tonic so powerful as expectation of something tomorrow."[80] Hope allows one to move from uncertainty to a higher probability of certainty. It bridges what could be and what is desired. It tempers the reality of the present unsatisfactory condition.

Thus far we have dealt with encouraging and uplifting forms of hope. However, other types of hope exist. We must monitor for false hope. We usually think of false hope as ensuring that a patient will get better, when he or she likely will not. However, in my experience, this type of false hope is far less common than the false hopelessness that is presented in such a way that despair is generated. That is the worst false hope.

> The worst false hope is the false hopelessness that is presented in such a way that despair is generated.

Eroding or disappearing hope occurs on bad hair days, when some event or some person takes away what the patient has clung to, or we become sick and tired of dealing with the complexities of the healthcare delivery system, like too many tests and exams and too many visits to the doctors. Sometimes, patients wonder if it will ever end. They think, "What if I go through this, and the cancer is still there? Is it worth it?"

Hope takes life on life's terms. We deal with the way it is today. We expect a better tomorrow. We deal with tomorrow when it gets here. As Joan Chittister, a Benedictine nun, wrote

> Hope is not a matter of waiting for things outside of us to get better. It is about getting better inside about what is going on outside. It is about becoming open to the God of Newness. It is about allowing ourselves to let go of the present, to believe in the future we cannot see but trust to God. Surrendering to the demands of the moment, holding on when holding on seems pointless, brings us to that point of personal transformation, which is the juncture of maturity and sagacity. Then, whatever the circumstances, however hard the task, the struggles of life may indeed shunt us from mountain top to mountain top but they will not destroy us.[81]

Perhaps the greatest understanding of cancer is hope.[82] Hope is the basis for treatment, and the reason for participating in clinical trials. Not only is hope an integral component for the patient, it is also a motivating force for the healthcare professions.

> Hope is the motivating force for healthcare professionals when dealing with tragic, life-threatening events.

You Still Have Hope

If you can look at the sunset and smile,
then you still have hope.
If you can find beauty in the colors of a small flower,
then you still have hope.
If you can find pleasure in the movement of a butterfly,
then you still have hope.
If the smile of a child can still warm your heart,
then you still have hope.
If you can see the good in other people,
then you still have hope.
If the rain breaking on a roof top can still lull you to sleep,
then you still have hope.
If the sight of a rainbow still makes you stop and stare in wonder,
then you still have hope.
If the soft fur of a favored pet still feels pleasant under your fingertips,
then you still have hope.
If you meet new people with a trace of excitement and optimism,
then you still have hope.
If you give people the benefit of a doubt,
then you still have hope.
If you still offer your hand in friendship to others that have touched
your life,
then you still have hope.
If receiving an unexpected card or letter still brings a pleasant
surprise,
then you still have hope.
If the suffering of others still fills you with pain and frustration,
then you still have hope.
If you refuse to let a friendship die,
or accept that it must end,
then you still have hope.
If you look forward to a time or place of quiet and reflection,
then you still have hope.
If you still buy the ornaments,
put up the Christmas tree or cook the supper,

then you still have hope.
If you can look to the past and smile,
then you still have hope.
If, when faced with the bad,
when told everything is futile,
you can still look up and end the conversation with the phrase …
"yeah … BUT,"
then you still have hope.
Hope is such a marvelous thing.
It bends, it twists, it sometimes hides,
but rarely does it break.
It sustains us when nothing else can.
It gives us reason to continue and courage to move ahead,
when we tell ourselves we'd rather give in.
Hope puts a smile on our face
when the heart cannot manage.
Hope puts our feet on the path
when our eyes cannot see it.
Hope moves us to act
when our souls are confused of the direction.
Hope is a wonderful thing,
something to be cherished and nurtured,
and something that will refresh us in return.
And it can be found in each of us,
and it can bring light into the darkest of places.
NEVER LOSE HOPE!

—Author unknown

We're in This Together

Virginia never once felt like she was going to die. She was not quite ready. Now, every day with her husband, Wayne, is a miracle. With a diagnosis of stage IV non-Hodgkin's lymphoma, she and her husband have grown closer and deeper in love than ever. Their story is one of love and triumph.

Recurrent Non-Hodgkin's Lymphoma

Virginia found swelling on both sides of her neck. It did not go away, and she saw a surgeon. A biopsy was done and revealed she had non-Hodgkin's lymphoma. When Virginia was first diagnosed, she had stage IV lymphoma, since her bone marrow biopsies showed malignant lymphoma as well. She also had widespread lymph node enlargement throughout her abdominal and pelvic areas. She also had an enlarged spleen. She underwent chemotherapy for eight cycles.

She had progressive disease within a year, and her chemotherapy was changed. After five cycles, she was again without evidence of disease and remained disease-free until four years ago. When the lymphoma recurred, she was treated on a clinical trial designed for relapsed lymphoma. She was treated with six cycles of chemotherapy followed by maintenance Rituxin. It has been over two years since she received any treatment, and she remains disease-free.

Her treatments were difficult. She experienced hospitalization for the side effects and had significant myelosuppression. She required multiple transfusions. She experienced a delayed recovery in her platelets.

It has been ten years since her initial diagnosis and almost three years since her last treatment. Virginia and her husband, Wayne, are always together. They have a trust in God and in each other. Both cherish the ability to bring joy to the other. They are an inspiration, both as individuals and as a married couple.

Virginia's Story with Her Husband Wayne

Virginia

Family is important to me. My mother and father moved back to this area when my grandfather became very ill. My father took care of him. When my parents became ill, I moved here to take care of them. I've been here about thirty-five years now. My husband and I made our life here.

Then, ten years ago, I was diagnosed with cancer. I did not even know I was sick. I was hanging out clothes one day, and I got so tired, I had to sit down. I could hardly go on. I noticed a lump that had come up around my collarbone area. I was rubbing my neck one night, and I pressed in a little further. It felt soft and spongy. It was very strange, so I called my doctor. He wanted to know how long it had been there. It had only been about a week or so. But he was very concerned and sent me to my surgeon, who did a biopsy.

The biopsy revealed it was non-Hodgkin's lymphoma. The cancer was everywhere. It was in my neck, my chest, and my spleen. I was diagnosed with stage IV lymphoma. I went through chemo for over six months. I took eight treatments of chemotherapy.

The cancer recurred after about a year. I did chemotherapy again, and I was in remission for three years. Then it came back a third time. We did chemo yet again, and now, I am in remission over two years. I think I have done about twenty-four months of chemotherapy all total.

But so far, everything is good, thank God. Except now I have shingles, and in many ways, it's worse than the cancer. It's right across my breast and under my arm and down my back. Talk about pain! It's awful. It will make you go insane if you let it. I am so thankful for the new shingles treatment.

But you can't feel sorry for yourself through all of this. We just figured we had to do what we had to do to fight it. You know it's there, and you have to do it. You need to continually have God in your heart and ask his guidance and just trust him with all your being. He will bring you through it.

> You learn to trust God, not for the desired outcome, but for the relationship.

And having cancer has brought my husband and me closer together and deeper in love. He is my cornerstone, one of them. God is the first, you know. Wayne, my husband, would bring me in for my treatments and sit with me a while. Then he would go back to work and come back to pick me up. He is retired now, so he has been right here for all the other treatments.

You can't pull apart from your spouse. You have got to continue to love each other. Be there for each other. We don't really do much, but whatever it is, we are together. We look at life differently now. Love is much deeper, much stronger.

Soul mates are what we are. He is my *everything*. He told me the other day, "You're here for me, and I am here for you." We do everything together. Right now we are making rugs. With little money for travel and so forth, we spend our time together.

> The best recipe for a good marriage
> is to spend time with each other.

At first, it was very, very scary. We did not know anything about what was going on or what the disease was. We didn't know anything about cancer or its treatment. It was just so overwhelming.

At one point, Wayne had a triple aortic aneurysm operation, and I stayed with him the entire time. But then I got sick again and had to go to the emergency room. I had an allergic reaction to one of the chemotherapy drugs. Some of the doctors thought I had a blood clot in my lungs. I couldn't breathe or talk, and they finally gave me oxygen. They put me in intensive care, the doctors scared me to death, saying they thought I had a blood clot in my lung, and it didn't look good for me. But I pulled through again.

I just said, "I am in your hands, God. Your will be done." I do not remember asking "Why me?" And Wayne joined me in that trust. Yes, it was rough getting through it. We just took it day by day, together. I never once felt that I was going to die. I just trusted my God and my doctors because I was not quite ready.

I also truly trust my doctors and all my nurses. They are fantastic. I call them my angels.

I am here for a reason. I don't know exactly for what purpose. One purpose is that we are here for each other. We take care of each other. Some tell us we are an encouragement to other couples to share their lives together and do things together. Fewer couples seem to be doing that. We are blessed by bringing each other joy.

> Mutual joy is often seen at the beginning of a relationship. It is refreshing to hear someone say, "We are blessed by bringing each other joy."

Wayne (Virginia's Husband)

You have to do what you have got to do. You know it's there, and you have to do it. You can't feel sorry for yourself. I mean you have got to continually have God in your heart and ask his guidance and just trust him with all your being. He will bring you through it. Every day is a new day for us.

> As we reconcile suffering and scripture, we discovered three important lessons:
> (1) Our thinking changed even if the suffering continued.
> (2) We learned to trust God, not for the outcome, but for the relationship.
> (3) We embraced suffering in that we ask God to use it to glorify him.

THE GIFT OF WENESS

How do I describe Virginia and Wayne? They are a beautiful couple who love each other dearly and who demonstrate commitment to their saying of "I do." What gift have they received? Initially, I thought about unity. But unity takes away individualism. What about intimacy? They have an intimacy, but they have more. After rereading their story several times, I realized the gift is one of togetherness. However, "togetherness" is simply insufficient to describe the magnitude of the gift. For that reason, the gift is best referred to as "weness," a term used by others to describe flourishing marriages.[83]

Virginia stated in reference to her cancer, "And it has brought my husband and me closer together and deeper in love." Virginia and Wayne used their struggles to grow closer together as wife and husband, and to persevere when facing trials and tribulations.

> Struggles can become the basis for intimacy.

Their growth is in contrast to many couples who are torn apart by difficult times, in general, and medical problems in particular. They demonstrate the strength of their marriage with their views on their life. As Virginia says, "We don't really do much, but whatever it is, we are together. We look at life differently now. Love is much deeper, much stronger."

When Virginia and Wayne are telling their story, they frequently refer to "we" and only occasionally refer to "me." They are always together, always sharing, living because of each other, and when one suffers, they both suffer. The gift of weness requires more than being connected emotionally and physically. It transcends these dimensions into the spiritual realm. Clearly, Virginia and Wayne have moved beyond adversity, and they did so within their relationship, which was founded and continues to improve based on their spiritual intimacy with God and with each other.

Virginia and Wayne have more than intimacy. Many types of intimacy exist, such as physical (generally viewed as sexual), emotional, intellectual, work, crisis, and spiritual.[84] The more types of intimacy a couple experiences, the more weness they receive. As a couple experiences and internalizes successive types of intimacy, weness becomes easier to receive.

Weness can never begin as a goal. It becomes a lifestyle, continuously improving a couple's relationship. What does such a relationship look like? Any relationship between two people is about how they relate to each other; that relationship's product becomes essential to their well-being. Based on the lives of Virginia and Wayne, let's examine several noticeable aspects of weness.

It goes without saying that, to receive the gift of weness, love must exist. But with the high divorce rate, perhaps it needs saying. Love is paramount to a good marriage. Not only the physical, sexual intimacy that often appears to be substituted for love, but the *agape* love that transcends the physical and emotional. Both are needed. It begins with a love whose origin is God and develops into physical intimacy. The process of love develops between two diverse individuals, and it is also the expression of such unity to the world.

To experience weness, trust is critical. Trust says, "I know you will not harm me, and I know you will assist me. And I will do the same for you." Trust, evidenced by interdependence, involves a "we are in this together" thought process. Cancer or other problems become not about "me" but about "us." One has compassion for the other and actually, as the derivation of the word indicates, suffers alongside the other. For a couple, maintaining trust is easier than to attempt to reclaim it. Lack of trust precludes the development

> Steps for the gift of weness:
> 1. Love
> 2. Trust
> 3. Mutual commitment
> 4. Use difficulties to enhance the relationship
> 5. Spend time together
> 6. Seek intimacy
> 7. Pursue a spiritually based life
> 8. Consider it a blessing to bring joy to another

of a strong marriage and hinders experiencing the gift of weness.

Commitment, a critical component of weness, must be mutual. Commitment depends on the stated obligations to each other. It is tested and proven during difficult times. Virginia and Wayne are committed to each other. Moreover, they are committed to the institution of marriage and its sanctity. Their spiritual foundation underlies their drive and determination.

> Commitment is tested and proved during difficult times.

The love and respect between spouses must be mutual. Couples show it by saying "we" instead of "me." They facilitate admiration, not by a good self-image, but by an image of self-respect. Respect shown to another is a demonstration to the world of how we value that individual. When demonstrated at home, it is demonstrated to the world.

Common goals, especially spiritual, are a vital component. Each individual in a marriage is progressing in his/her own journey, simultaneously participating in the the journey of the spouse. With a gift of weness, each spouse, with his/her own personal relationship with the spiritual, also participates in a greater dimension with the other spouse. The spiritual dimension allows a hope of togetherness far greater than the short-lived physical togetherness and superior to emotional intimacy. The spiritual allows a connectedness with others, with creation, with God, and the spiritual realm he has created.

The gift of togetherness shines as two people are in pursuit of life spiritually. Two diverse individuals, united in marriage, committed to forever marriage, grow spiritually. Each couple demonstrates a unique unity in diversity—a new "life" so to speak. Such a life becomes a testimony to others, perhaps to struggling couples, or to couples who wish to give up. As individuals mature in togetherness, the personal identities tend to be shaped by each other, and similarities dominate over differences. It is as if each is looking in the mirror and seeing unity rather than an individual.

Weness fulfills a need, a longing to be part of a successful and mutually beneficial group or society. Marriage, the traditional entity, has regrettably disintegrated, primarily due to lack of trust, so fewer and fewer couples will experience weness. John Gottman has studied marriage for many years, and the greatest predictor of a successful marriage, from early onset, is when marriage is dominated by "weness" and not "meness."[85]

Weness reflects the creation relationship. It is all about togetherness. God is together with Adam and then both Adam and Eve. There is an intimacy in their togetherness that is an example of what should be in store for us: a togetherness of communication as God walks and talks and provides. As human beings, we are responsible to God for care of Creation. God established reciprocity in his creation mandate. What he had made would provide for his children, and they would work to demonstrate their acceptance of this commission, and in so doing worship him.

Weness requires communication. We demonstrate human weness by caring for each other, doing things together, and being one. Creation responds to God with joy and delight. God gave his human creations the ability to make decision, and we must make the decision to reverse the thought from "It's all about me" to "It's all about you, God."[86] Weness may be as close as possible to "heaven experienced on earth."

MARRIAGE JOINS TWO PEOPLE
IN THE CIRCLE OF ITS LOVE[87]

Marriage is a commitment to life—
to the best that two people can find
and bring out in each other.
It offers opportunities for sharing and growth
that no other human relationship can equal,
a joining that is promised for a lifetime.
Within the circle of its love,
marriage encompasses all of life's most important relationships.
A wife and a husband are each other's best friend,
confidant, lover, teacher, listener, and critic.
There may come times when one partner is heartbroken or ailing,
and the love of the other
may resemble the tender caring of a parent for a child.
Marriage deepens and enriches every facet of life.
Happiness is fuller; memories are fresher; commitment is stronger;
even anger is felt more strongly, and passes away more quickly.
Marriage understands and forgives the mistakes life is unable to
avoid.
It encourages and nurtures new life, new experiences,
and new ways of expressing love through the seasons of life.

When two people pledge to love and care for each other in marriage
they create a spirit unique to themselves,
which binds them closer than any spoken or written words.
Marriage is a promise, a potential,
made in the hearts of two people who love,
which takes a lifetime to fulfill.

—Edmund O'Neill (1929)

Just Another Hill to Climb

For over thirty years, Phyllis has worked in the medical field. Diagnosed with breast cancer on Valentine's Day, Phyllis decided it would not get her down and she would come out on top, no matter what. She would not let cancer win. Today, Phyllis is "Super Nanny," watching her grandchildren every day as if nothing ever happened.

HER-2 POSITIVE BREAST CANCER

Some Valentine's Day! Phyllis was diagnosed with breast cancer. As a nurse, she knew she should have a mammogram but had always avoided having one. She changed primary care doctors, and he insisted she have a mammogram. The mammogram showed an abnormality of the left breast. She had no pain, swelling, soreness, or palpable mass. The biopsy revealed a 2.5 cm infiltrating ductal carcinoma. She underwent lymph node evaluation, and no cancer was in her lymph nodes. The breast cancer removed from her was estrogen positive and HER-2 positive. She had a lumpectomy.

She received chemotherapy for four cycles. She had many complications during her treatment. Her port-a-cath became infected and required removal. She has resistant staph infection. She developed *Clostridium difficle* toxic colitis due to the antibiotics to treat the methicillin resistant staph aureus infection. She was treated with radiation therapy after her chemotherapy was completed.

She was also placed on an oral antihormal therapy with treatment intended for five years. She was also treated with intravenous Herceptin for a year. Initially used for metastatic breast cancer, the addition of Herceptin (trastuzumab) to combination chemotherapy resulted in a significant decrease in the risk of recurrence of breast cancer. Patients are considered "Her-2-positive" if they make too much of HER-2. HER-2 is a protein found on the surface of some breast cancer cells. About 20 percent of the breast cancer make too much HER-2.The true story of the development of Herceptin was detailed in a book, *Her-2* by Robert Bazell, and a movie, *Living Proof.*

PHYLLIS'S STORY

I am fifty-one years old and in my second marriage. I have two boys, each of them has four children, and I had never been sick in my life. I have worked in the health-care field for more than thirty years, first as a certified pharmacy technician, and then as a nurse. I didn't work very long as a nurse because of blood clots in my legs, but I loved it when I did. Before cancer, I was only hospitalized four times: two to have my children and two for those blood clots.

I had always refused to have a mammogram even though my doctor kept telling me to get one. I didn't do it because I did my own breast exams and never found anything suspicious. Colleagues would tell me I needed a mammogram, and I would say, "Yeah, right." Then I changed primary care doctors, and he insisted I have a mammogram. I did. The mammogram had a suspicious area. It was my first mammogram. I am so thankful he insisted. The mass that was detected on the mammogram could not be felt by me or the physicians. The mass was about 2.5 centimeters in diameter, or about 1 inch. I went to see a surgeon, and he biopsied the area. I was diagnosed with breast cancer on Valentine's Day, almost three years ago. From February to May of that year, I had seven surgeries associated with my cancer.

I told my husband before I went to see the surgeon, "Now, get ready, because I know this is not going to be something good. I have dealt with patients, and I just know something is wrong by the way I feel."

He said, "You don't know that. We have to think positive."

I told my husband, "Well, I do think positive." I knew it would not be good, but I also knew in my heart something could be done about it.

My biopsy was scheduled for Valentine's Day, and of course, it wasn't a big deal. Initially the surgeon told us the mass wasn't malignant, but after a few days of pathology tests, I was called back in to the surgeon's office, and I thought, "Yeah, he has done found out something." He told me it was cancer, but it was so small, and he thought he got all of it. But still, he recommended a second surgery to make sure he didn't miss anything. He also removed the lymph nodes. That was the most pain I had. But it did not last long. Now, that was over and done with.

I had a port put in because my veins would collapse every time an IV was started. I had a lot of problems with the port because it came loose and moved, so it was difficult to access. Then I spent about two weeks in the hospital receiving antibiotics because the port became infected. Eventually, the surgeon replaced the port. I had more problems with the port than I did the cancer. When the first port was removed, due to the infection, the wound had to be left open, and I had to clean it with saline and pack it with gauze. It took about four weeks to completely heal.

The family had more difficulty accepting the complications with the port than with the surgery for cancer. They saw me suffering more. I also had *Clostridium difficule* infection of the intestine and had to take medication for that. I had a lot of diarrhea associated with that. I threw up my medicines. But you know, I got through it. I continued with my chemotherapy. After the chemotherapy, I was treated with trastuzumab (Herceptin), a monoclonal antibody, for one year. I also had thirty-eight radiation therapy treatments because I had a lumpectomy rather than a mastectomy.

As far as my children, you know how it is when mother gets sick. That's something major, especially when mother has never been sick. They handled it better than I thought they would. They didn't really talk to me about it. They avoided the subject and did not visit me while I was in the hospital. But they were around me at home when I was doing my chemotherapy.

My hair started coming out in handfuls, and I had to cut it. I probably lost about half of it. I told my husband, Scott, "If I end up with bald spots, I would shave my head." I did not want to go around looking pathetic.

Everybody asked me why I did not get really upset about my cancer. I thought part of it was probably my medical background. I have dealt with pain and suffering of others. But I have always been the type of person who comes out on top. Nothing gets me down. So when I found out that I had to have the chemotherapy, and my hair might come out, I just handled it. It was just another hill to climb. I made up my mind to just keep right on going.

I have had enough things happen in my life when I had asked "Why?" This was not one of those times. I went through a nightmare when a member of my family was involved in a shooting incident. I experienced firsthand in one day, one hospital scene, like out of a movie that changed my life forever. I was working in the emergency room when a shooting victim was brought in on a typical busy day. For some reason, I was so drawn to this family, and as the patient was worked on, I tried to console the other family member. I did not even know at the moment my own family member was in the next room waiting to see me because he was the reason the victim had been shot and was dying. As the story unfolded in a matter of minutes, I realized one must try to always be prepared for the unexpected. We do not have control over life's events, but we must make the best of it and learn something. I wasn't prepared, but I did learn a lot about communication and forgiveness. It was a senseless tragedy, which brought great suffering to several families. I know it probably helped prepare me and my family for my having breast cancer. Unexpected events in our lives do not have to break us; they can make us strong. We have to be there for each other. No matter what happens.

I faced breast cancer the same way I do everything in life. I said, "Okay, another hill to climb. One step at a time climbing up that hill with support and I know I will be able to knock it out. It's going to be over and done with." So when I had my last year's report on February 14, everything was free and clear. I felt I had reached the top of that hill with my support system and my faith.

I am an only child. I have always had to be the rock for everybody else. I knew that if I showed concern or broke down that my mom and dad could not have handled it. My husband is the same way. I am the glue that holds our family together. I knew better than to break down or get emotional about it. I had to dig down, grab the bootstraps, hang on, and just keep going.

Chemotherapy drags you down. You don't even want to move. But you have to keep moving. Radiation therapy doesn't hurt. You don't even know you're receiving it. You are there for a few minutes and then it's over. But chemotherapy makes you want to throw up your toenails. I was nauseated but did not vomit with chemotherapy. There were days I didn't feel like getting out of bed, but I got up and kept going. I kept my routine pretty well on track. I didn't have much of a taste for anything, but my mom kept encouraging me to eat. She would prepare whatever I thought I wanted. Sometimes I could eat it and sometimes not. I did not like being pampered and petted. Sometimes it was more than I could take, and I would just ask them to leave me alone for a few days. I felt like an invalid around them.

You must have faith in God, your doctors, your nurses, and yourself that you can pull through it, no matter what. My church prays weekly for me to stay well. They know I keep plugging away. Now, I would have broken down and cried every day if I thought it would help, but I knew it wasn't going to help anything. Crying was going to just hurt matters more, and I was one of the lucky ones, since I only had to take four cycles of the strong chemotherapy.

The hardest thing was trying to make my grandchildren understand I could not go out and play with them like I used to. But I am back to keeping three of them every day, so you know I am getting back into the swing of the "Nanny" thing. I keep a one-year-old, a three-year-old, and a four-year-old.

I try to encourage others. I tell them, "Look, I know it's scary. I have been there and done that." "Chemotherapy may drag you down and make you feel so bad that you will not want to even move. But you have to keep going." It will get better. The family of the patient needs to be positive. I was blessed to have a family that accepted my illness and had a positive mental attitude. Families need to remind the patients that they will get better. Focus on solutions, and not problems.

Cancer patients are so supportive of each other. It is like having another family at the clinic. We chitchat and get to know each other. We keep up with how each one is doing. We encourage one another. We provide and receive support. We are involved. It was important for me to keep a good attitude, to keep on fighting.

Everybody has a guardian angel, and mine is right here with me. I have a friend in Iraq who drives a truck and hauls jet fuel. This lady in Scanya, Iraq, makes these little pieces of jewelry. They are actually coins. The military personnel, every time they go through Scanya, buy some. My friend bought one for me shaped like a guardian angel and had it put on a chain. It says "Always with you" on the back, and it represents my guardian angel.

THE GIFT OF PERSEVERANCE

Phyllis saw her health problems as a potential for good when she remarked, "These unexpected events in our lives do not have to break us, but can make us strong. We have to be there for each other." "They know I just keep plugging away." Those unexpected events that slam us against the wall and result in us wanting to throw in the towel come at us from all angles. Don't quit. Persevere. The gift of perseverance, that continued pursuit of our goal, remains after the trauma or tragedy is all but gone. Persistence aids our survival. It means continuing to keep on despite obstacles. Napoleon Bonaparte said, "Victory belongs to the most persevering."[88] While victory cannot be guaranteed by perseverance, character formation can.

> Don't quit. Persevere. The end result
> is patience, experience and hope
> (Romans 5:4).

Within a few miles of our clinic stands a constant reminder about perseverance, the birthplace of America's first lady of courage, Helen Keller, who persevered though lacking the ability to speak, hear, or see. When visiting her birthplace and viewing the pump where she learned to spell W-A-T-E-R at the persistence of her teacher Anne Sullivan, I am overcome with the power of the gift of perseverance. Across the Tennessee River is yet another reminder of perseverance, the log cabin home of William Christopher Handy, Father of the Blues, who persevered in playing music, despite the wishes of his father, and gave us that form of music know as *the Blues*.

Perseverance is important in living life. How can we reach our God-given potential, either physically, emotionally, or spiritually, if we lack the ability to keep on keeping on? Perseverance in suffering leads to character formation (Romans 5:4). Perseverance, in addition to building character, also displays our character.

> It is through perseverance that our character is built.
> Perseverance is also the means of displaying our character.

Perseverance comes about when our faith is tested and completes its work, and we become mature (James 1:4).

Perseverance involves hard work. Often, we discuss persistence in reference to competitive sports, such as is seen in *Facing the Giants*,[89] but in Phyllis's case it refers to strength resulting from staying the course. Perseverance in our context does not involve competition. It involves living. We need a burning desire to live, perhaps to echo the words of Paul (2 Timothy 4:7). Perseverance is a desired characteristic for the productive life of a Christian (2 Peter 1:5–9).

Perseverance involves patience. Most of us remember the winner of the race between the tortoise and hare, or the little engine that could. Many of us can remember instances in our lives when we have recalled the moral of such a story and received encouragement. We need patience when we face medical problems, especially cancer. In addition to weekly visits to the clinic, patients face countless X-rays, scans, referral appointments, and hospitalizations. Their schedule is changed frequently.

Calvin Coolidge admonishes, "Press on! Nothing in this world can take the place of persistence. Talent will not; nothing is more common than unsuccessful people with talent. Genius will not; unrewarded genius is almost a proverb. Education will not; the world is full of educated derelicts. Persistence and determination alone are omnipotent." The slogan "press on" has solved and always will solve the problems of the human race.[90]

Steps to the gift of perseverance:
1. Focus on your goal
2. See the potential for good
3. Examine what character development is occurring
4. Exhibit persistent patience
5. Look for the spiritual component.

When Phyllis's friends and neighbors would ask why she did not appear upset about being diagnosed with cancer, her perseverance answered, "It was just another hill to climb. I made up my mind to just keep right on going." We receive the gift of perseverance more easily when we have previously faced difficulties. Phyllis had so many taxing times, trials, and tribulations in her life that she did not ask "Why me?" anymore.

> Facing previous trials is the only preparation we receive for perseverance.

Perseverance is often spiritual. As Phyllis says, "You have to have faith in God, your doctors, your nurses, and yourself that you can pull through it no matter what. My church prays weekly for me to stay well. They know I just keep plugging away." From a spiritual point of view, we can improve our perseverance by praying for help, reading God's word, aligning our lives with God's intent, and rejoicing in the opportunities to demonstrate perseverance.

Perseverance allows for encouragement. Phyllis can say to a cancer patient: "Look, I know it's scary. I have been there and done that." "But you have to keep going." "Focus on solutions, not problems." Phyllis, in turn, receives encouragement. Perseverance proves mutual. Every time we help another person, we receive benefit.

Persistence involves more than achieving a goal; it involves a lifestyle. If the goal is to live forever, then persistence is not realistic. If the goal is to live as well as you can, while living as long as you can, then persistence stays with us. As such, the gift of perseverance extends beyond actively fighting cancer.

Phyllis has a necklace with the inscription "Always with you" on it. Perseverance is like that. Phyllis, through multiple circumstances and events in her life, has received the gift of perseverance. Each time, she is able to keep on going, and she receives a little more. Phyllis had been through a difficult time with a loved one involved in a tragic shooting. This affected her heart more than the diagnosis of cancer. She knew if she could make it through the difficult time with her loved one, then she could go through this battle with cancer. Perseverance in the former had formed her character in the latter. Perseverance is just a part of her way of dealing with tragedy. Perseverance allows Phyllis a more abundant life.

I've Dreamed Many Dreams That Never Came True

I've dreamed many dreams that never came true,
I've seen them vanish at dawn;
But I've realized enough of my dreams, thank God,
To make me want to dream on.
I've prayed many prayers when no answer came,
I've waited patient and long;
But answers have come to enough of my prayers
To make me keep praying on.
I've trusted many a friend who failed
And left me to weep alone;
But I've found enough of my friends true-blue
To make me keep trusting on.
I've sown many seeds that fell by the way
For the birds to feed upon;
But I've held enough golden sheaves in my hand,
To make me keep sowing on.
I've drained the cup of disappointment and pain,
I've gone many days without song,
But I've sipped enough nectar from the rose of life
To make me want to live on.

— Author Unknown (referenced by Charles Allen, in *The Secret of Abundant Living*)

A Survivor's Ride
by Edie Hand

As a businesswoman with lots of personality, a wife, and mother, my life has always been filled with trials to triumphs. It is the rides through life that some of us seemingly go over more bumps and through bigger ole mud holes than others for longer periods of time. My "unexpected gift" with cancer has been the special relationships with my doctors, as well as finding a new compassion for my fellow man. Simply learning to listen and be a voice through the word for others.

I'm a Southern lady, Alabama born, but blessed to be worldly. Over the past thirty years, I have had occurrences of cancer along with a rare chronic bacterial disease. I am happy to say that I am a survivor. In between my battles with cancer of the kidney, breast, and uterus, my weight would yo-yo. I was either overweight or underweight, back to normal, and then a few months later I was twenty-five pounds overweight again. I was concerned about my weight with having a career in entertainment and public speaking. Speaking in front of a large audience and performing on my television show, I was conscious of my appearance and knew everyone else was also. Still, I struggled to control it.

I finally came to an understanding that what I really needed was to do much more than control my weight. I needed to achieve wholeness—a balance of spirit, mind, and body. I sought God's help in achieving this through prayer. As I prayed for wholeness, I gained strength, confidence, and knowledge that I would lose weight and find ways to keep it off. I started making better decisions on the food I ate. I learned as a cookbook author to cook lighter—reducing my overall intake of fat. I also became more aware of the overall amount of calories that I was getting in my diet. I reduced those. I started a simple exercise program and still strive to get more rest. For many years, I had sustained myself on a maximum of five hours of sleep per night. That was simply not enough. I further realized that just as there are important ingredients in a recipe, there are also important ingredients to life. I could be on a diet program, but if I didn't have a positive attitude and make the right lifestyle decisions about all aspects of my life, I was just applying a temporary fix.

When I was growing up, my days were filled with good food and good people. The family picnics held at my grandparents' house were fun times that included aunts, uncles, and cousins. My most famous cousin, Elvis Presley, and my great Aunt Minnie, Elvis's grandmother, shared in some of the good times of traditional Southern food and family fun. Now that I am an adult, I know I need the discipline of planning. The doctors, my husband, Mark, and my son, Linc, are my sources of encouragement to keep my positive attitude, including my come aparts with my continued battle for a healthier lifestyle. I know I want instant answers during tough health periods, so I ask for them in prayers. These answers come to me in different ways and forms to strengthen me to be tougher mentally. It helps with my continued efforts in maintaining my confidence one day at a time. Faith in God has carried me through some dark lonely hours. Although my life has had many dark moments, my faith has deepened.

All three of my brothers—David, Terry, and Philip Blackburn—have died young in tragic ways. Before my brother Terry passed, he asked me to tell our story, so I did in a recent novella, *The Last Christmas Ride*. Writing is another source for me in learning how to let go and just live. Our rides through life do have rough places. I can still hear my late grandmother Alice's words in my head, "Life will have rough rides and big ole mud holes along the way, but with faith and family you can survive well." My story is really your story too; we just never know when we are going to take our last ride. Do we? Experiences in life led me to understand that I needed to achieve a balance of wholeness of spirit, mind, and body. I now feel each day is a "gift of time." I see more clearly that when one door of happiness closes, another will open. I don't want to miss what God has in store for me today.

The Grand Finale: Consider carefully what you must do in the final hour of the day and what can be set aside. Let the advice of the scriptures ring true in your spirit: "God will take of your tomorrow, too. Live one day at a time" (Matthew 6:34). The way I see it—"We don't have control over our lives' events, but we do have control over how we respond to them."

A Physician's Journey
by J. Patrick Daugherty

From a nine-year-old boy talking to his grandfather the night of his death, and hearing him sing "Amazing Grace" as he died that night, to a man sitting across from his mother as she described finding a mass in her breast, cancer has impacted my life. Sometimes I can look back and see how past events have impacted my life. The two aforementioned did. At other times, I can experience an event and know it will impact my future. Such is the case of the twelve individuals profiled in this book.

I grew up in the mountainous region of southeast Tennessee. My family had lived there since the 1820s. We were a simple family. We did not have any health insurance. As a youngster witnessing the hardship this placed on my family to pay the bills, I swore I would never be without health insurance. My grandmother, too proud to receive government assistance, would barter her physician visits. Ol' Doc Epperson would exchange an office visit for a pint of corn relish. Little did I know that I would have the opportunity to return that deed to others in my practice of medicine. Every time I am able to do that, I recall my home, my family, and my simple way of life.

Mom had always said she would never take treatment if she had cancer. However, like the majority of people with such a diagnosis, she underwent surgery and chemotherapy. The will to live is one of the strongest forces to be reckoned with. The three-plus years she lived after her diagnosis were some of the best years of her life, and mine as well. I even helped her piece a quilt.

I never planned to be a physician. As a young teen, my goal was to be a professional wrestler. At sixteen, I fractured my hip and subsequently developed osteonecrosis. Because of this, I received assistance to go to college from the Tennessee Department of Rehabilitation. Keep in mind I graduated toward the bottom of my class from high school. When I enrolled at what is now Lee University, I was exposed to the joy of learning. After receiving a PhD and working in research at Oak

Ridge National Laboratory, I entered medical school at the University of Alabama in Birmingham with the intention of never practicing medicine. I simply wanted to do research. My life was not to turn out the way I envisioned. Patients were largely responsible for my change from a research physician to a practicing physician. I received much encouragement from the patients regarding my bedside manners and how beneficial I was to them to sit and listen, answer their questions, and maintain hope. Toward the end of my fellowship at Fox Chase Cancer Center in Philadelphia, a series of events occurred that resulted in me moving to northwest Alabama and establishing the first medical oncology practice in the area. That was in 1987.

I have been blessed to be accepted in this area, to have my family here, and to have as many friends as I do. I often think how brave our patients are, to put trust in a stranger who will give them potentially serious drugs. Yet week after week, often with a little encouragement, they return hoping for those words, "The cancer is shrinking." We laugh. We cry and we hug.

Gifts came from this struggling or suffering. The gifts the patients obtain cannot benefit me without a little struggle of my own. I know that each of these gifts goes a long way in living better. Yet they will never be internalized until put there by suffering that pierces the soul. Not all are touched this way and receive these gifts. It is part of our personality and training.

My most recent academic studies occurred at Gordon-Conwell Theological Seminary, in South Hamilton, Massachusetts. Yes, a patient was involved. A lady with colon cancer came to see me one day, and she had recently moved to the area from the Boston area. As we chatted and got to know each other, she encouraged me to pursue my goal at the seminary from which she had just retired. In a few weeks I was accepted and four years later was graduated with a doctor of ministry.

I am impatient. When I am having a difficult day, I can often recall the few words of a patient that has meant a lot to me, and expect that I will not suffer when in the middle of a trial or tribulation. That is not the way it works. I cannot fully internalize another's gift. The gift comes at a price. Suffering is process we go through and the price we pay for the ability to be a better person.

Some of the sayings I have learned from patients are "I don't have time to be mad." "Life is good, even when it's bad." "It's okay to cry—you just pee less." "Let go and let God." "Just turn it over to God." "Keep hoeing to the end of the row." "I can't, he can, let's go." "Here I am, use me." "Don't be a wimp for Jesus." "I'm living on bonus time." "Resolve your conflicts." "Don't waste time on self-pity." "Cancer is the best thing that ever happened to me." "Live today as if it is your last." "Live to leave a legacy." "Love transcends death." "Little peace but much hope." "A dirty house is desirable." "Write letters and pay bills." "Set goals." "Feel your feelings."

Each saying has become a pearl, an unexpected gift, forming a necklace, which is worn around my heart. Through these, I have learned how to live.

About the Authors

Dr. J. Patrick Daugherty can be described as one who enjoys life, appreciates opportunities, understands the significance of simplicity, and views work as his ministry. The vast extremes between his childhood in the Appalachian Mountains and his international opportunities as scientist, physician, and theologian speak to his abilities, ambition, and compassion for those less advantaged.

Patrick founded and currently directs the Northwest Alabama Cancer Center with offices in Florence and Muscle Shoals, Alabama, and is medical director of Hospice of Tennessee Valley in Florence. He continues to care for his many patients and is thought of as a man of compassion, boundless energy, and enthusiasm for life, by his patients, friends, and family.

Dr. Daugherty has been the principal investigator on grants from the National Science Foundation, National Cancer Institute, Kemp-Caraway Heart Institute, American Heart Association, and from numerous pharmaceutical companies. He has served on the grant review board of the National Cancer Institute and currently serves as member of the lung cancer study committee of Veeda Oncology. He has published numerous scientific studies and presented his results nationally and internationally, and recently presented a paper at Duke University at the Conference on Spirituality, Theology and Healthcare.

Patrick was named Alumni of the Year of Lee University and is an associate councilor of the Southern Medical Association. During the past year, he participated in three medical mission trips (Brazil and Honduras) and a pastors' conference (Honduras), volunteers at the La Clinica Christiana, Inc., a medical ministry targeting uninsured individuals in the northwestern Alabama area.

Although the first in his family to obtain a college education (BS, Lee University), he continued his love for learning by earning a PhD in biochemistry and radiation biology from the University of Tennessee, an MD from the University of Alabama in Birmingham, and a DMin from Gordon-Conwell Theological Seminary, South Hamilton, Massachusetts.

Patrick lives with his wife and childhood sweetheart, Becky, in Florence, Alabama. They have three daughters and seven granddaughters, who affectionately refer to him as "dada."

Edie Hand is one of those remarkable people who brightens up a room as soon as she walks in. Her philosophy for living life with gusto can be seen in everything she does, especially in her work as an acclaimed celebrity chef, author, philanthropist, speaker, and businesswoman.

Edie learned about the simple joys of family, life, and helping others from her modest childhood growing up in the rural south. She is a cousin to the late Elvis Presley and also the cousin of 2007 Nashville Star winner, Angela Hacker. She has authored, coauthored, and helped develop over twenty books. Her books range from inspirational, to cookbooks and novellas.

Edie has starred in national commercials and daytime television soaps. She has hosted numerous national radio and television shows and been the CEO of Hand 'N Hand Advertising, Inc., since 1976. Edie is a three-time cancer survivor and an advocate for cancer research. Edie is actively involved with American Women in Radio and Television, National Speakers Association, National Association of Women Business Owners, and has worked to benefit the Children's Hospital of Alabama, Children's Miracle Network, St. Jude Children's Research Hospital, Camp Smile-A-Mile, and Country Music Hall of Fame Foundation. She is a graduate of the University of North Alabama. Edie lives near Birmingham, Alabama, with her husband Mark Aldridge, an educator. Her only son, Linc Hand, a working actor, lives in Los Angeles, California.

For more information go to these Web sites:
www.ediehand.com
www.ediehandfoundation.org

Upcoming books with Edie Hand

Women of True Grit (March 2010)
How to Mop with Your Pearls On (2010)
ABC of Sales and Sales Etiquette (2010)
36 Things to Enhance Your 11-14 Year Old's Self-Esteem (2010)
Sisterhood Ride (September 2010)

Endnotes

1. Leah Ingram, "Gifts and Etiquette," Gifts and Etiquette Q&A, Updated for 2009, **http://www.giftsandetiquette.com/** (accessed July l, 2009).

2. Paul McFedries, "Word Spy. The Word Lover's Guide to New Words," Regift, **http://www.wordspy.com/words/regift.asp** (accessed July 1, 2009).

3. The ExmaxHealth Home Page, "Spirituality and Healing," Most Americans Believe in God But Views of Deity Vary, **http://www.emaxhealth.com/9/7768.html** (accessed June 29, 2009).

4. C. S. Lewis, *The Problem of Pain* (New York: HarperOne, 2001), 91.

5. C. S. Lewis, *A Grief Observed* (New York: HarperOne, 1989).

6. Brother Lawrence, *Practicing His Presence,* ed. F. Laubach (Jacksonville, Florida: Seedsowers Christian Book Publishing House, 1988).

7. Bill W., "Bill's Story" in *Alcoholics Anonymous,* 3rd ed. (New York: Alcoholics Anonymous World Services, Inc., 1976), 1–16.

8 William James, *The Varieties of Religious Experience: A Study in Human Nature. Being the Gifford Lectures on Natural Religion Delivered at Edinburgh in 1901–1902* (New York: The Modern Library, Random House, Inc., 1994), 24.

9. Kenneth I. Pargament, *The Psychology of Religion and Coping: Theory, Research, Practice* (New York: Guilford Press, 1997).

10. Kenneth I. Pargament, Harold G. Koenig, Nalini Tarakeshwar, and June Hahn, "Religious Struggle as a Predictor of Mortality among Medically Ill Elderly Patients: A 2-year Longitudinal Study," *Arch. Intern. Med.* 161, no. 15 (2001): 1881–1885.

11. Julie J. Exline and Ephraim Rose, "Religious and Spiritual

Struggles," *Handbook of the Psychology of Religion,* eds. R. F. Paloutzian and C. L. Parks (New York: Guilford, 2005), 315–330.

12. B. S. Cole, C. M. Hopkins, J. Tisak, C. I. Steel, and B. I. Carr, "Assessing Spiritual Growth and Spiritual Decline Following a Diagnosis of Cancer: Reliability and Validity of the Spiritual Transformation Scale," *Psycho-oncology* 17, no. 2 (2008): 112–121.

13. J. P. Daugherty, W. Messenger, and H. W. Robinson, "Enhanced Spiritual Transformation in Cancer Patients Following Intervention with Peer Patient Narratives." Presented at the meeting of the society for spirituality, theology, and health. Duke University, Durham, NC. June 25–27, 2008. **http://www.societysth.org/resources/pdfs/daughertyabstract.pdf** (accessed July 1, 2009).

14. St. Jude Children's Research Hospital, "Leukemias / Lymphomas: Acute Lymphoblastic Leukemia (ALL)," **http://www.stjude.org/stjude/v/index.jsp?vgnextoid=4c5b061585f70110VgnVCM1000001e0215acRCRD&vgnextchannel=7f87ef9e87018010VgnVCM1000000e2015acRCRD** (accessed June 29, 2009).

15. The story of the founding of St. Jude Children's Research Hospital involves an unwanted gift in a way. Young Danny Thomas, a struggling entertainer with seven dollars in his pocket, prayed before a statue of St. Jude Thaddeus in a Detroit church. He prayed a question: "Show me my way in life." Later, during another turning point in his life, he promised to build a shrine to St. Jude. As Danny and Marie Thomas were blessed, they extended that blessing to countless others. For example, Austin, if diagnosed in 1962, would have had a five-year survival 4 percent, whereas today it is 94 percent. This organization of faith continues its goal of treating children with catastrophic illnesses. Treatment is provided to all patients. It is the only pediatric research center where families are not asked to pay more than what is covered by their insurance. If the patient lacks insurance, the treatment is provided without charge. At one time, they treated everyone for free. Danny Thomas knew the importance of helping others. He found his meaning and purpose to living. "All of us are born for a reason, but all of us don't discover why. Success in life has nothing to do with what you gain in life or accomplish for yourself. It's what you do for others." ThinkExist, "Danny Thomas Quotes," **http://thinkexist.**

com/quotation/all of us are born for a reason-but all of us don/339486.html (accessed June 29, 2009).

16. *Alcoholics Anonymous,* 3rd ed. (New York: Alcoholics Anonymous World Services, Inc., 1976), 85.

17. Karl Paul Reinhold Niebuhr (1892–1971) was a Protestant theologian. He openly opposed Hitler and was vocal against the inhumane conditions of assembly line employment as well as the Ku Klux Klan. In 1964, he was awarded the Presidential Medal of Freedom by President Lyndon Johnson. The original version of the Serenity Prayer was apparently associated with a sermon he gave on practical Christianity and was eventually modified and has been used by Alcoholics Anonymous since the early 1940s, and subsequently by many twelve-step programs. Reinhold Niebuhr Place, the section of 120th Street between Broadway and Riverside Drive in New York City, was named in his honor. The Union Theological Seminary is located here. AA History, "The Origin of the Serenity Prayer," **http://www.aahistory.com/prayer.html** (accessed June 29, 2009).

18. V. T. DeVita, T. S. Lawrence, S. A. Rosenberg, R. A. DePinho, and R. A. Weinberg, eds., *DeVita, Hellman, and Rosenburg's Cancer: Principles & Practice of Oncology,* 2 vols., 8th ed. (New York: Lipincott Williams & Wilkins, 2008).

19. People of faith will sometimes view the need for an antidepressant as a weakness on their part. A lot of time in the clinic is spent helping such patients realize that it is not a sign of weakness. It is a sign of the effects of stress on the levels of various chemicals in the brain. Annette, a woman of faith, realizes the importance of this medicine.

20. W. R. Miller and J. C'de Bacva, *Quantum Change: When Epiphanies and Sudden Insights Transform Ordinary Lives* (New York: The Guilford Press, 2001). Also, see end note 5.

21. Pope John Paul II, *On Human Work: Laborem Exercens* (Boston: Pauline Books and Media Publishing House, 1981), 55.

22. Ibid., 57.

23. Brenda Ladun, *Getting Better, Not Bitter: A Spiritual Prescription for Breast Cancer* (Birmingham, Alabama: New Hope Publishers, 2002).

24. John R. Durant, personal communication, 2009.

25. EWTN, Global Catholic Network, "Her Words," **http://www. ewtn.com/MotherTeresa/words.htm** (accessed June 29 2009).

26. "Mother Teresa—The Path of Love," **http://home.comcast. net/~motherteresasite/mother.html** (accessed June 29 2009).

27. J. Martin, "A Saint's Dark Night," *New York Times*, August 29, 2007, **http://www.nytimes.com/2007/08/29/opinion/29martin. html** (accessed June 29, 2009).

28. Harold S. Kushner, *When Bad Things Happen to Good People* (New York: Avon Books, 1981).

29. American Rhetoric, "Rhetoric of 9-11," **http://www. americanrhetoric.com/speeches/billygraham911memorial.htm** (accessed June 29, 2009).

30. Desiring God, God-Centered Resources from the Ministry of John Piper, "Thank You Lord for Solzhenitsyn," **http://www.desiringgod. org/Blog/1336 thank you lord for solzhenitsyn/** (accessed June 29, 2009).

31. Quotations Book, "Mother Theresa," **http://quotationsbook.com/ quote/37909/** (accessed June 29, 2009).

32. Quote Land, "Suffering," **http://www.quoteland.com/topic. asp?CATEGORY ID=292** (accessed June 29, 2009).

33. Chicken Bones: A Journal, "The Legacy of Martin Luther King, Jr.," **http://www.nathanielturner.com/legacyofmartinlutherking. htm** (accessed June 29, 2009).

34. "The Dick Staub Interview: Brennan Manning on Ruthless Trust," *Christianity Today*, **http://www.christianitytoday.com/ct/2002/ decemberweb-only/12-9-21.0.html** (accessed June 29, 2009).

35. J. Claypool, *Tracks of a Fellow Struggler: Living and Growing Through Grief* (Harrisburg, Pennsylvania: Morehouse Publishing, 2004), 88.

36. Wikipedia, "Shawdowlands," **http://en.wikipedia.org/wiki/ Shadowlands** (accessed June 29, 2009).

37. Viktor E. Frankl, *Man's Search for Meaning* (Boston: Beacon Press, 2006).

38. A Personal Message from Hans Selye, **http://www.joe.org/ joe/1980may/80-3-a1.pdf** (accessed June 29, 2009).

39. The Ralph Waldo Emerson Society, " Success," **http://www.cas.**

sc.edu/engl/emerson/ephemera/success.html. This poem has been attributed to Emerson. However, it was written by Bessie Anderson Stanley in 1904 (accessed June 29, 2009).

40. O. Chambers, *My Utmost for His Highest,* ed. J. Reiman (Grand Rapids, MI: Discovery House Publishers, 1992).

41. See endnote 7, 63.

42. J. P. Daugherty, "Spiritual Intervention in Newly Diagnosed Cancer Patients Undergoing Chemotherapy" (Thesis, DMin, Gordon-Conwell Theological Seminary, 2007).

43. D. B. Beaton, Effects of Stress and Psychological Disorders on the Immune System, **http://www.personalityresearch.org/papers/beaton.html** (accessed June 29, 2009).

44. Pam's experiences occurred prior the use of the current class of antiemetic drugs, which have resulted in a dramatic decrease in the incidence of chemotherapy-induced nausea and vomiting.

45. ThinkExit. "Mahatma Gandhi quotes," **http://thinkexist.com/quotation/there is nothing that wastes the body like worry/169608.html** (accessed June 29, 2009).

46. The Quotation Page, "Haddon Robinson," **http://www.quotationspage.com/quote/1673.html** (accessed June 29, 2009).

47. Ernest Kutz and Katherine Ketcham, *The Spirituality of Imperfection: Storytelling and the Search for Meaning* (New York: Bantam, 1992).

48. Wikipedia, "The Lion King," **http://en.wikipedia.org/wiki/The Lion King** (accessed June 29, 2009).

49. New Advent, "St. Francis of Assisi," **http://www.newadvent.org/cathen/06221a.htm**. Roman Catholic Friar St. Francis of Assisi (September 26, 1182–October 3, 1226) founded the Order of Friars Minor (Franciscans). Known as the patron saint of animals, birds, and the environment, St. Francis lived a carefree life into early young adulthood, until he experienced a spiritual crisis in 1204, when a serious illness left him, like many of us, searching for a worthy cause. He felt compassion for the lepers. Although born rich he chose to experience poverty. Regarding suffering, he wrote: "We have no right to glory in ourselves because of any

extraordinary gifts, since we may glory in crosses, afflictions and tribulations, because these are our own" (accessed July 1, 2009).

50. American Cancer Society, "Prevention and Early Detection," **http://www.cancer.org/docroot/ped/content/ped 2 3x acs cancer detection guidelines 36.asp**, National Cancer Institute, "Prostate Cancer Screening," **http://www.cancer.gov/ cancertopics/pdq/screening/prostate/HealthProfessional/ allpages** (accessed June 30, 2009). American Society of Clinical Oncology, "Trends in Screening for Prostate Cancer," **http://www. asco.org/ASCOv2/Meetings/Abstracts?&vmview=abst detail view&confID=65&abstractID=32815** (accessed June 29, 2009). "The Prostate Cancer Screening Controversy Continues," *Chicago Tribune,* **http://newsblogs.chicagotribune.com/triage/2009/03/ the-prostate-cancer-screening-controversy-continues.html** (accessed June 29, 2009).

51. T. W. Smith, Spiritual and Religious Transformations in America: The National Spiritual Transformation Study, **http://www-news. uchicago.edu/releases/05/121305.norc.pdf** (accessed June 29, 2009).

52. C. S. Carver and M. H. Antoni, "Finding Benefit in Breast Cancer during the Year after Diagnosis Predicts Better Adjustment 5 to 8 Years after Diagnosis," *Health Psychology* 23 no. 6 (2004): 595–598.

53. B. Cole and K. Pargament, 1999. "Re-Creating Your Life: A Spiritual/Psycho-Therapeutic Intervention for People Diagnosed with Cancer," *Psycho-Oncology* 89 no. 5 (1999): 395–407.

54. L. Nash and S. McLennan, *Church on Sunday, Work on Monday: The Challenge of Fusing Christian Values with Business Life* (San Francisco: Jossey-Bass, A Wiley Company, 2001).

55. J. D. Koss-Chioino and P. Hefner, *Spiritual Transformation and Healing: Anthropological, Theological, Neuroscientific, and Clinical Perspectives* (New York: Altamira Press, 2006).

56. D. Willard, *Renovations of the Heart: Putting on the Character of Christ* (Colorado Springs, CO: NavPress, 2002), 69.

57. See endnote 6.

58. ThinkExist, "Robert Francis Kennedy Quotes," **http://thinkexist.**

com/quotation/tragedy is a tool for the living to gain wisdom/224056.html (accessed June 29 2009).

59. R. H. Conwell, *Acres of Diamonds* (New York: Jove, 1986).

60. V. P. Collins, *Acceptance* (St. Meinrad, Indiana: Abby Press, 1960).

61. *Alcoholics Anonymous*, 449.

62. The Voice of Love, "The Serenity Prayer," http://www. thevoiceforlove.com/serenity-prayer.html (accessed July 2, 2009).

63. Philippians 4:8–9.

64. Inspiration Speak, "Daily Acceptance Prayer," http://www. inspirationpeak.com/cgi-bin/poetry.cgi?record=143 (accessed July 2, 2009).

65. Weil Lifestyle, "Does Attitude Affect Cancer Survival?" http:// www.drweil.com/drw/u/id/QAA326565 (accessed June 29, 2009).

66. MedicineNet, "Attitude Doesn't Affect Cancer Survival," http:// www.medicinenet.com/script/main/art.asp?articlekey=84723 (accessed June 29, 2009).

67. Pamela J. Goodwin, Molyn Leszcz, Marguerite Ennis, Jan Koopmans, Leslie Vincent, Helaine Guther, Elaine Drysdale, Marilyn Hundleby, Harvey M. Chochinov, Margaret Navarro, Michael Speca, Julia Masterson, Liz Dohan, Rami Sela, Barbara Warren, Alexander Paterson, Kathleen I. Pritchard, Andrew Arnold, Richard Doll, Susan E. O'Reilly, Gail Quirt, Nicky Hood, and Jonathan Hunter, "The Effect of Group Psychosocial Support on Survival in Metastatic Breast Cancer," *NEJM* 345 no. 24(2001):171901726, http://content.nejm.org/cgi/content/ abstract/345/24/1719 (accessed June 29, 2009).

68. Linda E. Carlson and Barry D. Bultz, "Benefits of Psychosocial Oncology Care: Improved Quality of Life and Medical Cost Offset," *Health and Quality of Life Outcomes* 1 no. 8: 2003, http:// www.hqlo.com/content/1/1/8 (accessed June 29, 2009).

69. Deborah D. Danner, David A. Snowdon, and Wallace V. Friesen, "Positive Emotions in Early Life and Longevity: Findings from the Nun Study," http://www.apa.org/journals/features/psp805804. pdf (accessed June 29, 2009).

70. K. Pitkala, M. Laakkonen, T. Strandberg, and R. Tilvis, "Positive Life Orientation as a Predictor of 10-year Outcome in an Aged Population," *Journal of Clinical Epidemiology* 57 no. 4 (2004): 409–414.

71. L. Gonzales, *Deep Survival. Who Lives, Who Dies, and Why* (New York: W. W. Norton & Company, 2005).

72. J. M. Robieng, E. M. Crimmins, S. Horiuchi, and Yi Zeng, eds., *Human Longevity, Individual Life Duration, and the Growth of the Oldest-old Population* (New York: Springer, 2007).

73. H. G. Koenig, M. E. McCullough, and D. B. Larson, *Handbook of Religion and Health* (Philadelphia: Templeton Foundation Press, 2001).

74 J. E. Gillham, "The Science of Optimism and Hope. Research Essays in Honor of Martin E. P. Seligman. Seligman, E. E. P. Optimism, Pessimism, and Mortality," *Mayo Clinic Proceedings* 75: 133–134, 2000.

75. T. Maruta, R. C. Colligan, M. Malinchoc, and K. P. Offord, Optimists vs Pessimists: Survival Rate among Medical Patients over a 30-year Period. *Mayo Clinic Proceedings* 75: 140–143, 2000.

76. Becca R. Levy, Martin D. Slade, Suzanne R. Kunkel, and Stanislav V. Kasl. "Longevity Increased by Positive Self-Perceptions of Aging," **http://www.apa.org/journals/releases/psp832261.pdf** (accessed June 30, 2009).

77. BellaOnline, The Voice of Women, "Attitude Poetry," **http://www.bellaonline.com/articles/art38590.asp** (accessed July 2, 2009).

78. J. Groopman, *The Anatomy of Hope: How People Prevail in the Face of Illness* (New York: Random house, 2003), xiv.

79. EnglishClub, "Hope springs eternal in the human breast," **http://www.englishclub.com/ref/esl/Sayings/H/Hope springs eternal in the human breast 672.htm** (accessed June 30, 2009).

80. LeadershipAudio, "Wise Old Sayings Remain True in Modern Times," **http://www.leadershipaudio.com/wise-old-sayings.html** (accessed June 30, 2009).

81. 30 Good Minutes, "The Spirituality of Hope," **http://www.csec.org/csec/sermon/Chittister 4613.htm** (accessed June 30, 2009).

82. TOUCH, Today Our Understanding of Cancer is Hope, L. Josof, 1982, Guidelines for organizing TOUCH, ACS, Alabama Division.

83. J. Gottman, *The Marriage Clinic* (New York: W. W. Norton & Company, 1999) **http://www.wcg.org/lit/booklets/families/ marriage1.htm** (accessed June 30, 2009).

84. O. Andrews and D. Andrews. *Husbands and Wives: The Best of Friends* (Nashville: Lifeway, 1994) **http://www.thefellowship.info/ Files/Resources/Intimacy-in-Marriage** (accessed June 30, 2009).

85. John Gottman, *The Marriage Clinic*. See note 83.

86. R. Warren, *The Purpose Driven Life: What on Earth Am I Here For*? (Grand Rapids: Zondervan, 2005).

87. WeddingReferences, "Poetry on Marriage," **http://www.wedding-references.com/poetry on marriage.htm** (accessed July 2, 2009).

88. QuotesDB, "Napoleon Bonaparte," **http://www.quotedb.com/ quotes/280** (accessed June 30, 2009).

89. Vic Johnson, "The Persistence Test," **http://www.vicjohnson. com/2007/03/01/the-persistence-test/** (accessed June 30, 2009).

90. The Quotation Page. "Calvin Coolige," **http://www. quotationspage.com/quotes/Calvin Coolidge/** (accessed June 30, 2009).